Gateways to Psychology

CONCEPT MAPS AND CONCEPT REVIEWS TWELFTH EDITION

Shawn Talbot

Kellogg Community College

Christine M. Vanchella

WADSWORTH
CENGAGE Learning

Australia • Brazil • Japan • Korea • Mexico • Singapore • Spain • United Kingdom • United States

WADSWORTH
CENGAGE Learning™

Gateways to Psychology: Concept Maps and Concept Reviews, **Twelfth Edition**
Shawn Talbot / Christine M. Vanchella

Senior Editor, Psychology: Jaime Perkins

Development Editor: Jeremy Judson

Assistant Editor: Ileana Shevlin

Editorial Assistant: Sarah Worrell

Technology Project Manager: Rachel Guzman

Executive Marketing Manager: Kimberly Russell

Marketing Manager: Tierra Morgan

Marketing Assistant: Molly Felz

Executive Marketing Communications Manager: Talia Wise

Sr. Content Project Manager, Editorial Production: Pat Waldo

Creative Director: Rob Hugel

Art Director: Vernon Boes

Print Buyer: Karen Hunt

Image Permissions Manager: Mandy Groszko

Text Permissions Manager: Bobbie Broyer

Production Service: Julie Ninnis, Graphic World Inc.

Text Designer: Liz Harasymczuk

Photo Researcher: Kathleen Olson

Cover Designer: Liz Harasymczuk

Cover Image: Nick Wienholt

Compositor: Graphic World Inc.

For product information and technology assistance, contact us at
Cengage Learning Customer & Sales Support, 1-800-354-9706.

For permission to use material from this text or product, submit all requests online at **www.cengage.com/permissions**. Further permissions questions can be e-mailed to **permissionrequest@cengage.com**.

ISBN-13: 978-0-495-82929-4
ISBN-10: 0-495-82929-3

Wadsworth
10 Davis Drive
Belmont, CA 94002-3098
USA

Cengage Learning is a leading provider of customized learning solutions with office locations around the globe, including Singapore, the United Kingdom, Australia, Mexico, Brazil, and Japan. Locate your local office at **international.cengage.com/region.**

Cengage Learning products are represented in Canada by Nelson Education, Ltd.

For your course and learning solutions, visit **www.cengage.com.**
Purchase any of our products at your local college store or at our preferred online store **www.iChapters.com.**

Printed in Canada

3 4 5 6 7 12 11 10 09

contents

to the student

This booklet is a study tool designed to help you better understand essential chapter concepts. For each chapter, this booklet provides the Chapter Concepts, a visual guide of key topics, and a Concept Review consisting of 35 multiple-choice quiz questions per chapter.

Visual Guides

Research has shown that, for some learners, presenting information in a visual format improves retention of material. The visual guides began several years ago with an individual instructor's attempt to give students a study tool in an alternative format that allowed them to review information as they prepared for examinations. You will read about the concept of cognitive mapping in Chapter 7, Conditioning and Learning, and about how educational psychologists attempt to improve the quality of learning in Chapter 18, Applied Psychology. Many of you will find the visual guides extremely helpful from the very beginning of your course. For others, you may discover their value as you proceed with your studies.

How do you make use of these visual guides? The Introduction to the main text discusses how to study psychology and explains the SQ4R method. (A quick synopsis is also provided here.) These visual guides are an integral part of the "S" ("Survey") and two of the "Rs" ("Reflect" and "Review").

Survey

Even before you survey the chapter, survey the visual guides. A preview such as this gives you an overview of what material will be covered and highlights some key concepts that you will want to focus on.

Reflect

The visual presentation demonstrates how one key topic relates to another. You may be surprised to see how many concepts are interconnected, and the visual guides provide an overview of these connections. Your long-term retention of the material can be improved by having an understanding of how the material you are studying relates to other material. The material in the visual guides is generally laid out in a top-down, left-to-right format. However, as you will see, the fact that most concepts are interrelated makes the exact layout of no great consequence.

Review

After you have read the chapter, when you want to test your mastery of the material, use the visual guides for review. At each point along the way, ask yourself:

- How much do I now know about each topic discussed here?
- What information do I now know that was not included in the visual guide?
- What items would I have added if I had been the creator of the visual guide?
- What questions is my instructor likely to ask about the topics that have been presented?

Some students may find it helpful to make detailed notes directly on the visual guides as they progress through the chapters.

Concept Review

In addition to the Chapter Concepts and visual guides of key concepts, you will find a chapter quiz consisting of 35 multiple-choice questions in each chapter. You can find additional quizzing and tutorial help at the text companion website, at www.cengage.com/psychology/coon.

We hope that you find these visual guides and Concept Review content to be valuable study tools in mastering your course material.

PSYCHOLOGY

The **science** of psychology is the study of behavior and mental processes using an empirical approach. The **profession** of psychology is the sharing and application of psychological knowledge. Psychologists follow a professional code of ethics that stresses competency, integrity, respect for privacy, and protection of the client's welfare.

Goals of Psychology

Psychologists gather information to benefit humanity. All research is aimed at fulfilling one or more of the **four goals of psychology:**
1. Describe: to name and classify the nature of behaviors
2. Understand: to know the "why" of behaviors
3. Prediction: to forecast future behaviors
4. Control: to alter conditions that affect behavior

Critical Thinking

To reach the goals of psychology requires critical thinking. Common-sense beliefs are often incorrect or even contradict scientific research. Although all information, from whatever source, should be evaluated critically, the media are particularly likely to contain inaccurate information. Beware of pseudo-psychologies.

Scientific Method

To conduct their research, psychologists use the **scientific method,** which is a very powerful way to observe the natural world and to form **valid conclusions** about human behavior.

History and Contemporary Perspectives

Early psychology included the approaches of structuralism, functionalism, behaviorism, Gestalt, psychoanalysis, and humanism. Modern psychology is shaped by the biological, psychological, and sociocultural perspectives.

Picture Partners/Alamy

1. Make Observations

Psychologists are observers. Events in the natural world prompt them to want to understand relationships in behavior. Observations prompt asking questions and seeking answers.

2. Define the Problem

A specific area to be addressed is defined in a logical manner.

3. Propose a Hypothesis

Based on what has been observed thus far, the psychologist creates a tentative, testable explanation of an event or relationship. Abstract concepts are operationally defined.

4. Gather Evidence / Conduct Research

The hypothesis is tested using a research method.

5. Publish Results

Research results must be public to promote discussions, debate, and replication. New theories are formed, and new areas of research are suggested.

6. Formulate Theory

A theory summarizes the existing data, explains them, and guides future research. The process begins again, incorporating what has been discovered.

Naturalistic Observation

Studies the behaviors of human and animals in natural settings.

Correlational Method

Takes measurements to discover the relationship between two events that appear to be connected.

Clinical Method

Reviews accidents or natural events that have affected an individual (or groups of individuals).

Survey Method

Asks questions about human behavior, thoughts, and attitudes.

Experimental Method

Designs a structured, controlled environment. The controls established by the formal experimental method are the best method for determining cause-and-effect relationships in psychology.

CHAPTER 1

Introduction to Psychology and Research Methods

Mike Nelson/AFP/Getty Images

Chapter Concepts

- *Psychology is the science of behavior and mental processes. Psychologists gather scientific data to describe, understand, predict, and control behavior.*
- *Psychologists are professionals who create and apply psychological knowledge.*
- *The scientific method is a powerful way to observe the natural world and draw valid conclusions.*
- *Psychological research begins with observations, questions, and hypotheses. Next, researchers gather evidence, test hypotheses, and publish results. Scientific debate and theories suggest new hypotheses that lead to further research.*
- *Experiments are the best way to identify cause-and-effect relationships in psychology.*
- *Critical thinking is central to the scientific method, psychology, and to effective behavior in general.*
- *Television, magazines, and other popular media are rife with inaccurate information. It is essential to critically evaluate information from popular sources—or from any source, for that matter.*
- *Psychological researchers make every effort to maintain high ethical standards in their work.*

Concept Review

1. *Psychology is defined as the scientific study of _____.*
   a. human behavior
   b. the mind
   c. behavior and mental processes
   d. mental processes

2. *Which is an example of an overt behavior?*
   a. thinking
   b. planning
   c. writing
   d. problem solving

3. *People who believe that a new diet is safe and effective because a doctor wrote the book are forgetting that*
   a. few "truths" transcend the need for testing.
   b. evidence varies in quality.
   c. authority does not automatically make an idea true.
   d. critical thinking requires an open mind.

4. *A psychologist whose interests lay in reasoning, problem solving, and memory is probably a*
   a. developmental psychologist.
   b. learning psychologist.
   c. social psychologist.
   d. cognitive psychologist.

5. *_____ psychologists are interested primarily in how psychological patterns of human behavior evolved and were inherited over the course of history.*
   a. Comparative
   b. Evolutionary
   c. Cultural
   d. Bio

6. *Which of the following is NOT one of the goals of psychology?*
   a. description
   b. understanding
   c. persistence
   d. control

7. *Introspection turned out to be a poor way to answer many questions because*
   a. Wundt would not allow others to use it without permission.
   b. it was difficult to determine what answers were correct.
   c. it was based on viewing only observable behaviors.
   d. it only examined perception.

8. *What did functionalism contribute?*
   a. It became the basis of behaviorism.
   b. It promoted educational psychology.
   c. It influenced the development of psychoanalysis.
   d. It argued that only humans should be the subjects of study.

9. *Behaviorism is the study of*
   a. covert behavior.
   b. consciousness.
   c. overt, observable behavior.
   d. introspection.

10. *Using learning principles to change problem behavior is known as*
    a. cognitive behaviorism.
    b. behavior therapy.
    c. Pavlovian conditioning.
    d. Skinner boxing.

11. *The Gestalt viewpoint has especially influenced studies of*
    a. behaviorism.
    b. psychopathy.
    c. personality and perception.
    d. psychoanalysis.

12. *Humanism stresses*
    a. unconscious forces.
    b. free will.
    c. environmental control.
    d. determinism.

13. *Which of the following major perspectives in psychology would measure the amount of blood flow to various parts of the brain during a letter-detection task?*
    a. psychodynamic
    b. behaviorist
    c. biopsychological
    d. cognitive

14. *The tendency to believe positive or flattering descriptions of yourself is also known as*
    a. cognitive dissonance.
    b. critical understanding.
    c. the Barnum effect.
    d. uncritical acceptance.

15. *Which of the following would be studied by a researcher in the field of positive psychology?*
    a. factors that reduce violence and aggression
    b. the role of conformity in riots
    c. the factors that may enhance an individual's creativity
    d. the factors that reduce job burnout among employees

16. *Which of the following is stressed in the professional code of ethics?*
    a. personal morality
    b. high levels of competition
    c. respect for people's right to privacy
    d. research protocols with humans only

17. *_____ refers to an ability to reflect on, evaluate, compare, analyze, critique, and synthesize information.*
    a. Critical thinking
    b. Decisive cognition
    c. Cognitive intelligence
    d. Analytical thought

18. *Operational definitions consist of*
    a. a tentative explanation of an event or relationship.
    b. the exact procedures used to represent a concept.
    c. controlled observations.
    d. results that can be replicated.

19. *The difference between a theory and a hypothesis is*
    a. a hypothesis makes tentative predictions about behavior; a theory summarizes existing research.
    b. a theory makes predictions about behavior; a hypothesis summarizes existing research.
    c. a hypothesis is an observation of behavior; a theory is the procedure used in an experiment.
    d. a hypothesis is used by other researchers to guide future research; a theory is a tentative explanation for a particular event.

20. *When an observer sees only what he or she expects to see, this is called*
    a. observational record.
    b. the observer effect.
    c. the anthropomorphic fallacy.
    d. observer bias.

21. *The weight of a horse jockey is probably _____ correlated with their ability to win races.*
    a. positively
    b. negatively
    c. not
    d. minimally

22. *Which correlation coefficient indicates the weakest relationship between variables?*
    a. +.89
    b. +.21
    c. −.75
    d. −.56

23. *Which of the following is an advantage of the experimental method?*
    a. high degree of control
    b. allows prediction
    c. not susceptible to coincidence
    d. confirms cause and effect

24. *Dr. Psychosomatic is investigating the effects of violent cartoon programs on children's aggressive play behavior. She has one group of 4-year-olds watch a 30-minute tape of a children's cartoon containing violence and another group of children the same age watch a nonviolent cartoon for the same length of time. Then she has trained observers watch the children at play and obtain aggression scores for each child. In this example, the dependent variable is*
    a. the aggression scores.
    b. the violent tape.
    c. the nonviolent tape.
    d. the 4-year-olds.

25. *The procedure by which each subject in a study has an equal chance of being assigned to the experimental and control group is called*
    a. random sampling.
    b. random assignment.
    c. an extraneous variable.
    d. meta analysis.

26. *Animal studies have been used by some psychologists in order to*
    a. discover principles that apply to animals.
    b. discover principles that apply to humans.
    c. better understand the mental illnesses of canines.
    d. increase funding levels.

27. *Joe takes an herbal supplement for pain in his knees. A few days after starting the supplement, his pain seems to decrease and he tells people that this supplement is wonderful at controlling knee pain. What else could explain Joe's diminished pain?*
    a. the placebo effect
    b. the replication effect
    c. the experimenter effect
    d. the observer effect

28. *If neither the subjects nor the experimenter know which subjects get the true independent variable and which get the placebo, the study is called a _____ experiment.*
    a. single-blind
    b. double-blind
    c. field
    d. dual

29. *Dr. Williams wants to find out how middle-class America feels about taxes. She goes to Neiman-Marcus and surveys the customers there. What has she done wrong?*
    a. She is questioning the government.
    b. She needed to have written questions.
    c. She failed to get a representative sample.
    d. She fell victim to the placebo effect.

30. *A prediction that prompts people to act in ways that make the prediction come true is known as*
    a. experimenter effect.
    b. social desirability.
    c. observer bias.
    d. self-fulfilling prophecy.

31. *Which of the following is one of the three major ethical issues to which researchers must be sensitive?*
    a. deception
    b. financial burden
    c. inconsequential harm
    d. invasion of personal beliefs

32. *Pseudopsychologists differ from mainstream psychologists in that*
    a. the former look for evidence to contradict their hypotheses.
    b. the former obtain results derived from the scientific method.
    c. the latter take advantage of the Barnum effect.
    d. the latter look for evidence to contradict their hypotheses.

33. *_____ believed that our behavior is deeply influenced by unconscious thoughts, impulses, and desires.*
    a. Wundt
    b. Freud
    c. Piaget
    d. Shiveana

34. *The U.S. Army slogan, "Be All You Can Be" might be considered an example of*
    a. self-evaluation.
    b. determinism.
    c. eclecticism.
    d. self-actualization.

35. *Palmistry and phrenology would both be examples of*
    a. parapsychology.
    b. cognitive psychology.
    c. pseudopsychology.
    d. psychoanalysis.

BIOPSYCHOLOGY

Nerve cell activity is the source of all experience and behavior. Psychologists who study how processes in the body, brain, and nervous system relate to behavior are called **biopsychologists.**

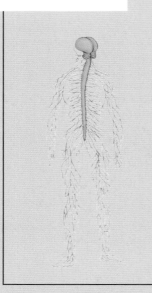

Neurons

All sensations, thoughts, feelings, motives, behaviors, and memories stem from brain activity. Neurons are composed of the **soma, axon, dendrites**, and **axon terminals**. Action potentials stimulate communication via **neurotransmitters** across a **synapse**.

Central Nervous System

The brain and the spinal column form the **central nervous system (CNS).**

Peripheral Nervous System

All the parts of the nervous system outside the brain and the spinal cord form the **peripheral nervous system (PNS).** It contains two subsystems.

Endocrine System

Endocrine glands form a second communication system in the body. Chemicals called **hormones** are secreted directly into the bloodstream or lymph system via the endocrine system.

Neuroplasticity and Neurogenesis

The brain's circuitry is not static. The brain grows new nerve cells and can "rewire" itself in response to changing environmental conditions.

The Brain

The brain is the largest center of nerve cell activity. Brain activities and structures are associated with all human capacities.

The Spinal Cord

The spinal cord connects the brain to other parts of the body, but it also does some computing on its own, as with **reflex arcs.**

Somatic Nervous System

Carries messages to and from the sense organs and skeletal muscles, generally controlling voluntary behaviors.

Autonomic Nervous System

Serves internal organs and glands. Comprised of **sympathetic** and **parasympathetic** branches.

CHAPTER 2

Brain and Behavior

Mapping Brain Structure and Function

Modern technology allows researchers to make bioelectrical recordings and computer-generated images of brain activity, thus gaining additional insight into how the brain works. Biopsychologists attempt to determine which areas of the brain are responsible for specific behaviors.

Cerebral Cortex

The cerebral cortex consists of two large **hemispheres** covering the upper part of the brain, connected by the **corpus callosum.** The hemispheres, which are specialized, are divided into four lobes: **frontal, parietal, temporal, and occipital.**

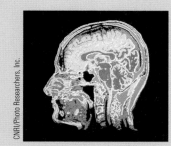

CNRI/Photo Researchers, Inc.

Subcortex

The subcortex consists of the **hindbrain, midbrain,** and lower parts of the **forebrain**. It contains many crucial brain structures necessary for survival.

Hill Street Studios/Photolibrary

Chapter Concepts

- *Biopsychologists study how processes in the body, brain, and nervous system relate to behavior.*
- *Ultimately, all behavior can be traced to the activity of nerve cells.*
- *To map the brain, researchers activate or disable specific areas and observe changes in behavior.*
- *Bioelectrical recordings and computer-generated images of brain activity provide additional insights into how the brain works.*
- *Sensations, thoughts, feelings, motives, actions, memories, and all other human capacities are associated with brain activities and structures.*
- *Endocrine glands serve as a chemical communication system within the body. Behavior is greatly influenced by the ebb and flow of hormones in the bloodstream.*
- *Brain dominance and brain activity determine if you are right-handed, left-handed, or ambidextrous.*
- *The brain's circuitry is not static. The brain grows new nerve cells, and it can "rewire" itself in response to changing environmental conditions.*

Concept Review

1. *The study of how biological processes relate to behavior is called*
   a. physiology.
   b. psychology.
   c. biopsychology.
   d. physiopsychology.

2. *Which of the following parts of a neuron is responsible for carrying information away from one end of a neuron to the other?*
   a. dendrite
   b. axon
   c. soma
   d. axon terminal

3. *Which is the message-receiving part of the neuron?*
   a. dendrite
   b. axon
   c. soma
   d. axon terminal

4. *Another name for the nerve impulse is the*
   a. resting potential.
   b. action potential.
   c. threshold.
   d. ion channel.

5. *An action potential is likely to occur when*
   a. the neuron reaches its resting potential.
   b. the neuron reaches threshold.
   c. potassium ions enter into the axon.
   d. the negative after-potential is reached.

6. *What happens at the synapse?*
   a. The neuron touches the next neuron, releasing its message.
   b. An electrical message jumps from one neuron to the next.
   c. The neuron extends cilia to the receiving neuron.
   d. The neuron releases chemicals called neurotransmitters onto the surface of the receiving neuron.

7. *Receptor sites are found on which of the following?*
   a. dendrites
   b. terminal branches
   c. nucleus
   d. none of the above

8. *Myelin is*
   a. a fatty layer coating the axon.
   b. a bundle of neuron fibers.
   c. the space between two neurons.
   d. a feeling of uneasiness.

9. *An example of a neuropeptide is*
   a. serotonin.
   b. dopamine.
   c. enkephalins
   d. acetylcholine

10. *Which part of the nervous system is being utilized as you sit in class and write your notes?*
    a. somatic
    b. autonomic
    c. sympathetic
    d. parasympathetic

11. *Which division of the nervous system is the "fight or flight" system?*
    a. somatic
    b. autonomic
    c. sympathetic
    d. parasympathetic

12. *Which technique for studying the brain involves the destruction of brain cells with an electrical current?*
    a. ablation
    b. deep lesioning
    c. EEG
    d. MRI

13. *A(n) _____ works by injecting radioactive glucose to determine which areas of the brain are most active during a task.*
    a. CT scan
    b. PET scan
    c. MRI
    d. EEG

14. *The left hemisphere is responsible for*
    a. pattern recognition.
    b. drawing pictures.
    c. detecting and expressing emotions.
    d. language and math.

15. *Susan was in an accident and experienced brain damage resulting in her having problems understanding spoken words. It is probable that she damaged which part of her brain?*
    a. the frontal lobe
    b. Broca's region
    c. Wernicke's area
    d. the temporal lobe

16. *Which of the following is TRUE about the somatosensory area?*
    a. The larger the area devoted to a particular body part, the more refined the movement.
    b. The larger the area devoted to a particular body part, the more sensitive the part of the body.
    c. The smaller the area devoted to a particular body part, the more refined the movement.
    d. It is an association area of the brain.

17. *A person who has difficulty with word expression, saying "seep" instead of "sleep," probably has damage to*
    a. Broca's area.
    b. Wernicke's area.
    c. the cerebral cortex.
    d. corpus callosum.

18. *With regard to the motor cortex, which of the following would get more area of cortex devoted to its functioning?*
    a. ear
    b. nose
    c. hand
    d. shin

19. *An inability to recognize familiar faces is known as*
    a. aphasia.
    b. agnosia.
    c. facial agnosia.
    d. unilateral neglect.

20. Which of the following is most vital to survival?
    a. medulla
    b. occipital lobe
    c. Wernicke's area
    d. Joshua's region

21. Which brain area is damaged if a person experiences loss of coordination and balance?
    a. medulla
    b. pons
    c. cerebellum
    d. reticular formation

22. Which brain area is involved in sleep and arousal, and connects the lower brain to the upper brain?
    a. medulla
    b. pons
    c. cerebellum
    d. reticular formation

23. If the _____ is damaged, you can lose your hearing, sight, sense of touch, or taste.
    a. hippocampus
    b. amygdala
    c. hypothalamus
    d. thalamus

24. Damage to the _____ might result in amnesia.
    a. hippocampus
    b. amygdala
    c. hypothalamus
    d. thalamus

25. Damage to the _____ might result in poor temperature regulation or disorders of appetite, sleep, or sex.
    a. hippocampus
    b. amygdala
    c. hypothalamus
    d. thalamus

26. Which part of the brain seems associated with fear and anger?
    a. hippocampus
    b. amygdala
    c. hypothalamus
    d. thalamus

27. This lobe of the brain is primarily involved with receiving visual information.
    a. frontal
    b. temporal
    c. occipital
    d. parietal

28. A split-brain patient, if presented with a picture of a dog to the left visual field and a cat to the right visual field, will draw _____ with their right hand.
    a. a cat
    b. a dog
    c. both a cat and a dog
    d. nothing

29. The endocrine system releases _____ that go directly _____.
    a. pheromones; into the air
    b. pheromones; into the bloodstream
    c. hormones; into the air
    d. hormones; into the bloodstream

30. When the pituitary secretes too much growth hormone late in the growth period, it can cause
    a. dwarfism.
    b. thyroidal confusion.
    c. acromegaly.
    d. premature puberty.

31. The master gland, controlled by the hypothalamus, is the
    a. pituitary.
    b. pineal.
    c. thyroid.
    d. adrenal gland.

32. A person who is thin, tense, nervous, and excitable might have an overactive
    a. adrenal gland.
    b. pituitary.
    c. gonad.
    d. thyroid.

33. Which of the following is true about the hormone melatonin?
    a. Higher levels cause drowsiness.
    b. Our bodies release more melatonin during daylight hours.
    c. Levels peak in the morning.
    d. It is released by the adrenal glands.

34. Plasticity of the brain means that the brain
    a. is soft to the touch.
    b. is unchanged by experience.
    c. is capable of changing its structure and functions.
    d. is easily damaged.

35. Caleb threw his tennis racquet after losing the match. This expression of anger most likely originated in what part of the brain?
    a. pons
    b. pineal gland
    c. parietal lobe
    d. limbic system

HUMAN DEVELOPMENT

Developmental psychology is the study of progressive changes in behavior and abilities at every stage of life. Principles of development help us understand our own behavior and that of others.

Reprinted with permission of Nelson Prentiss.

Sarah Putnum/Index Stock Imagery/Photolibrary

Tony Freeman/PhotoEdit

Nature vs. Nurture

Human development is an interaction of **heredity** (nature) and **environment** (nurture). Genetics gives each person potentials and limitations. Environmental deprivation and enrichment can influence these. Heredity, environment, and one's own behavior interact to determine one's **developmental level.**

Infancy and Childhood

Infancy and early childhood are critical times for physical, emotional, and cognitive development.

Adolescence and Young Adulthood

Adolescence is a culturally defined period between childhood and adulthood. Humans address many important developmental concerns during this time.

Psychosocial Dilemmas Across the Lifespan

Erikson describes the "typical" developmental tasks and life crises occurring at eight stages in life. Each stage confronts us with new **developmental tasks** that must be mastered for optimal development.

Later Adulthood

Well-being in adulthood is associated with self-acceptance, positive relations with others, autonomy, environmental mastery, life purpose, and personal growth. People do not necessarily experience a midlife crisis. Periods of stability are interspersed with transitions throughout the lifetime.

Death and Dying

Research by **thanatologists** shows a general pattern to the processes of terminal illness and death. Knowledge and understanding of these patterns can be very helpful.

CHAPTER 3

Human Development

Infant Development

Infants come into the world with senses, simple reflexes, and perceptual abilities. Emergence of basic motor and emotional abilities is influenced by **maturation**. Emotional development is heavily dependent on emotional **attachment** to the caregiver.

Parenting

Parents, as caregivers, play a critical role in development. **Authoritarian, permissive, and authoritative parenting styles** are associated with different child outcomes.

Language

Development of language proceeds through a series of stages. Caregivers shape development through **parentese** and feedback.

Cognitive Development

Piaget proposed that children's cognitive abilities develop through a series of stages. **Vygotsky** emphasized the **sociocultural** nature of cognition.

Puberty and Identity

The biological event of **puberty** occurs during adolescence, resulting in rapid physical growth and sexual maturity. The search for **identity** can be complicated and may be taking longer today than in the past.

Moral Development

Kohlberg proposed that moral development occurs through a series of stages from childhood to adulthood. Acquired values, beliefs, and thinking abilities guide responsible behavior.

Gary Conner/Index Stock Imagery/Photolibrary

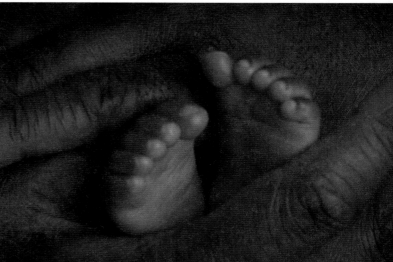

Paul Kuroda/Superstock

Chapter Concepts

- *You are a product of your genetic heritage and the environments in which you have lived.*
- *Infant development is strongly influenced by heredity. However, environmental factors such as nutrition, parenting, and learning also are important.*
- *All areas of child development are affected by conditions of deprivation and enrichment.*
- *Forming an emotional bond with a caregiver is a crucial event during infancy.*
- *Learning language is a cornerstone of early intellectual development.*
- *Piaget's stage theory provides a valuable map of how thinking abilities unfold.*
- *Vygotsky's theory reminds us that a child's mind is shaped by human relationships.*
- *Effective child discipline is consistent, humane, and encouraging and is based on respectful communications.*
- *Genetic research is making it possible to control some hereditary aspects of human reproduction, development, and behavior.*

Concept Review

1. Which of the following sequences is correct, from smallest unit to largest?
   a. genes, DNA, chromosomes
   b. DNA, genes, chromosomes
   c. chromosomes, genes, DNA
   d. genes, chromosomes, DNA

2. When a gene is _____, the feature it controls will appear every time the gene is present.
   a. dominant
   b. recessive
   c. passive
   d. polygenic

3. Which term refers to many genes working together to produce a trait or feature?
   a. dominant
   b. recessive
   c. passive
   d. polygenic

4. Brandon has a hot temper, broods a lot, and is rather disagreeable. He is probably
   a. an easy child.
   b. slow to warm up.
   c. difficult.
   d. none of the above

5. Ann is restrained and shy. She is probably what kind of child?
   a. an easy child
   b. slow to warm up
   c. difficult
   d. none of the above

6. A woman exposed to measles in early pregnancy has a child who is mentally retarded, whereas her sister, who was in the last months of pregnancy when exposed, has a normal child. This illustrates the concept of
   a. sensitive periods.
   b. genetic disorder.
   c. senescence.
   d. intrauterine periods.

7. Denny was born weighing only five pounds, with a small head, thin upper lip, and oddly shaped eyes. He is also a person with mental retardation. Denny's mother most likely used which of the following during her pregnancy?
   a. cocaine
   b. nicotine
   c. alcohol
   d. aspirin

8. Which of the following is not considered a teratogen?
   a. caffeine
   b. alcohol
   c. tobacco
   d. prenatal vitamins

9. Which of the following is an example of reciprocal influences in development?
   a. IQ is affected by genetics.
   b. IQ is affected by environmental factors, such as schooling.
   c. A child inherits a genetic potential for IQ, which can be reached only if they receive the proper stimulation from the environment, which they are also affecting.
   d. Heredity and environment have separate effects on intelligence.

10. A newborn's startle reflex is also called
    a. grasping.
    b. rooting.
    c. Moro.
    d. Babinski.

11. A neonates' best visual acuity is at approximately
    a. six inches.
    b. one foot.
    c. two feet.
    d. none of the above

12. A baby gains control of its neck muscles, then its arms, and finally its legs. This is called _____ development.
    a. proximodistal
    b. cephalocaudal
    c. specific to general
    d. gross to specific

13. Concerning maturation, although rate _____, order _____.
    a. is slow, is inconsistent.
    b. varies, varies less.
    c. stays consistent, changes.
    d. varies, stays constant.

14. All human emotions appear by
    a. 10 weeks.
    b. age 1.
    c. 6 months.
    d. Experts do not yet agree on how quickly emotions emerge.

15. Karen cries when her mother leaves the room. This is an example of
    a. social referencing.
    b. imitation.
    c. catharsis.
    d. separation anxiety.

16. In Ainsworth's study, a baby who seemed disinterested in the mother's comings and goings, turning away from her when she returned, was labeled
    a. securely attached.
    b. insecure-ambivalent.
    c. insecure-avoidant.
    d. disorganized.

17. An infant who experiences separation anxiety but is comforted when his mother returns can be labeled as having what type of attachment?
    a. insecure-ambivalent
    b. insecure-avoidant
    c. disorganized
    d. secure

18. Harlow's monkeys preferred the soft, clothe-covered surrogate mother monkey to the wire monkey providing food. This preference can best be explained by what term?
    a. contact comfort
    b. imprinting
    c. social referencing
    d. emotional attachment

19. Which of the following is NOT one of the things parents should look for in good quality day care?
    a. small number of children per worker
    b. trained caregivers
    c. small overall group size
    d. frequent staff turnover to prevent boredom

20. Affectional needs include which of the following?
    a. need for food
    b. need for water
    c. need for love
    d. all of the above

21. _____ refers to discrimination or prejudice based on age.
    a. Accommodation
    b. Ageism
    c. Elder abuse
    d. Elder stereotyping

22. Erik Erikson believed the first psychosocial task was that of:
    a. autonomy vs. shame and doubt.
    b. identity vs. role confusion.
    c. trust vs. mistrust.
    d. denial vs. acceptance.

23. Which is considered to be the most beneficial style of parenting?
    a. authoritarian
    b. authoritative
    c. permissive
    d. negligent

24. Which of the following techniques would an authoritative parent be most likely to use?
    a. power assertion
    b. withdrawal of love
    c. management techniques
    d. affection

25. What does Chomsky assert about language development?
    a. Humans have a genetic predisposition for language development.
    b. Language development is entirely a learned or environmental process.
    c. Humans utilize numerous patterns in creating their first sentences.
    d. Language development has no relationship to genetics.

26. In which level of Kohlberg's theory of moral reasoning would a person be if they seek to uphold their own morals, regardless of the consequences?
    a. preconventional
    b. conventional
    c. postconventional
    d. none of the above

27. An exaggerated pattern of speaking that parents use when talking to infants is referred to in the text as
    a. motherese.
    b. telegraphic speech.
    c. cooing.
    d. babbling.

28. According to Piaget, object permanence develops in the _____ stage.
    a. sensorimotor
    b. preoperational
    c. concrete operational
    d. formal operational

29. Which of the following is NOT one of Kübler-Ross's stages of death and dying?
    a. denial
    b. anger
    c. bargaining
    d. frustration

30. Emily sees a butterfly floating across her back yard, points and says, "Birdie!" Piaget would refer to this process as
    a. assimilation.
    b. accommodation.
    c. object permanence.
    d. approximation.

31. Puberty is _____ defined, whereas adolescence is defined by _____.
    a. biologically, culture
    b. culturally, biology
    c. environmentally, hormones
    d. physically, environment

32. _____ is the study of progressive changes in behavior and abilities, involves every stage of life from conception to death.
    a. Progressive psychology
    b. Lifespan science
    c. Humanism
    d. Developmental psychology

33. The physical growth and development of the body, brain, and nervous system is also referred to as
    a. maturation.
    b. readiness.
    c. physiological developmentalism.
    d. none of the above

34. Environment is to heredity as _____ is to _____.
    a. cognition, behavior
    b. nurture, nature
    c. love, hate
    d. physiology, psychology

35. Emily's parents considered the use of stimulating colors, sounds, and textures when decorating her nursery. This would be considered an example of a(n) _____ environment.
    a. child friendly
    b. overstimulating
    c. enriching
    d. depriving

SENSATION

Sensory systems link us to the external world and shape the flow of information to the brain. **Psychophysics** studies the relationship between physical stimuli and the sensations they evoke in the observer.

Sensory Systems

The external world produces a vast amount of data that could flood our senses. Sensory systems act as data-reduction systems, using processes of **transduction, sensory analysis, sensory coding,** and **sensory localization.**

Vision and Light

The eyes and the brain form a complex system for sensing the visible spectrum of light. Vision is based on an active, computer-like analysis of light patterns.

Hearing and Sound

Hearing involves an elaborate series of events through which sound waves are transduced, beginning with funneling in the **pinna** and ending with the detection of waves by tiny hair cells in the **cochlea. Conductive hearing loss** and **sensorineural hearing loss** affect many people.

Chemical Senses

Olfaction (sense of smell) and **gustation** (sense of taste) involve responses to molecules in the air or in food. Both senses have survival value and add pleasure to life.

Somesthetic Senses

The **skin senses, kinesthetic senses,** and **vestibular senses** help us feel and navigate within our environment.

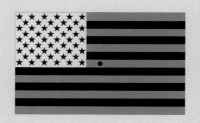

Perceptual Defenses

Psychophysical studies measure the minimum amount of energy necessary for sensation to occur. How an individual privately experiences the external stimuli depends on many factors. Emotions and motivations affect thresholds of perception.

Filtering Information

Many sensory events never reach awareness because of filtering processes. Incoming sensations may be affected by **sensory adaptation, selective attention,** or **sensory gating.**

Olfaction

A variety of smell receptors inside the nose identify various odors. Responses to odors are very individualized. Humans may be sensitive to **pheromones.**

Gustation

Taste receptors on the tongue and inside the mouth detect four or five basic tastes. Biology and experience influence taste preferences.

Skin Senses

Our skin provides us with information about touch, pressure, pain, cold, and warmth. Sensitivity to each is related to the number of receptors found in the skin. Free nerve endings can also produce these sensations.

Kinesthetic and Vestibular Senses

The kinesthetic sense monitors body position and movement through receptors in the muscles and joints. The vestibular sense provides information about the body's position in space through receptors in the inner ear. **Motion sickness** may be the result of conflicting visual, kinesthetic, and vestibular sensations.

CHAPTER 4

Sensation and Reality

Eyes

Visual photoreceptors are found in the retina. The **rods** and **cones** have different specializations, and they differ in color sensitivity.

Visual Defects

Visual problems include **myopia**, **hyperopia**, **presbyopia**, **astigmatism**, and **color blindness.**

Pain

There are different types of pain, and pain can be reduced or controlled by altering factors that affect its intensity.

Tim Flach/Getty Images

Chapter Concepts

- *Sensory systems select, analyze, and transduce information from the surrounding world and send it to the brain.*
- *Private sensations do not correspond perfectly to external stimuli. Studies in psychophysics relate physical energies to the sensations we experience.*
- *The eyes and the brain form a complex system for sensing light. Vision is based on an active, computer-like analysis of light patterns.*
- *All of the senses rely on a complex series of mechanical, chemical, and neural events to convert stimuli into messages understood by the brain.*
- *Sensory adaptation, selective attention, and sensory gating significantly modify our experiences. Only a small part reaches the brain or registers there.*
- *Pain can be reduced or controlled by altering factors that affect pain intensity.*

JSC/NASA

Concept Review

1. A device, such as the eye, that converts energy from one system to another is a(n)
   a. data reduction system.
   b. transducer.
   c. electromagnetic system.
   d. phosphene.

2. The conversion of important features of the world into a form that can be understood by the brain is called
   a. sensory analysis.
   b. sensory coding.
   c. localization of function.
   d. feature detection.

3. If you press on your eyelids, you will "see" colors and flashes of light. If you receive a blow to the side of your head, you will "hear" ringing. Which term best describes these phenomena?
   a. sensory analysis
   b. sensory coding
   c. sensory localization
   d. feature detection

4. The absolute threshold of smell
   a. stays consistent between situations.
   b. is consistent between first degree relatives.
   c. is one drop of perfume in a three-room apartment.
   d. differs from person to person.

5. A change in stimulus intensity that is detectable to an observer is
   a. a hertz.
   b. an absolute threshold.
   c. a difference threshold.
   d. a just noticeable difference.

6. Information processed below the normal threshold of awareness is called
   a. subliminal.
   b. supraliminal.
   c. the just noticeable difference.
   d. transient detectability.

7. You answer your phone and immediately recognize the voice of your best friend. What process is involved in this recognition?
   a. perception
   b. sensation
   c. perceptual expectancy
   d. the just noticeable difference

8. The term indicating the basic color categories is
   a. hue.
   b. saturation.
   c. brightness.
   d. color.

9. What part of the eye does most of the focusing in on an image?
   a. retina
   b. cornea
   c. photoreceptors
   d. pupil

10. Which kind of visual impairment is also called nearsightedness?
    a. hyperopia
    b. myopia
    c. presbyopia
    d. astigmatism

11. Which of the following refers to the misshaping of the cornea or lens?
    a. hyperopia
    b. myopia
    c. presbyopia
    d. astigmatism

12. What part of the eye would be the equivalent of film in a camera?
    a. cornea
    b. pupil
    c. lens
    d. retina

13. Which of the following types of cells produce color sensations and work best in bright light?
    a. rods
    b. cones
    c. ganglia
    d. amacrine

14. The spot on the retina where the optic nerve leaves the eye is called the
    a. blind spot.
    b. fovea.
    c. bipolar cell.
    d. amacrine layer.

15. Which of the following is responsible for the greatest visual acuity?
    a. blind spot
    b. fovea
    c. bipolar cell
    d. amacrine layer

16. In opponent-process theory, colors are perceived
    a. by two kinds of cones.
    b. by three kinds of rods.
    c. by rods and cones working together.
    d. by processing colors as "either-or" messages.

17. The trichromatic theory of color applies to
    a. the retina.
    b. the optic pathways.
    c. the thalamus.
    d. the visual cortex.

18. What type of light does NOT affect dark adaptation?
    a. white
    b. red
    c. green
    d. All light affects dark adaptation.

19. Pitch corresponds to _____, while loudness corresponds to _____.
    a. frequency; amplitude
    b. amplitude; frequency
    c. frequency; length of a sound wave
    d. length of a sound wave; amplitude

20. Which part of the ear concentrates or funnels sound waves?
    a. pinna
    b. tympanic membrane
    c. auditory ossicles
    d. cochlea

21. *What is the true organ of hearing that contains tiny hair cells that detect waves in the cochlear fluid?*
    a. pinna
    b. tympanic membrane
    c. auditory ossicles
    d. cochlea

22. *Where would you find the malleus?*
    a. outer ear
    b. middle ear
    c. inner ear
    d. olfactory cluster

23. *If the eardrum or ossicles are damaged, you might suffer from _____ hearing loss.*
    a. conductive
    b. nerve
    c. stimulation
    d. overload

24. *Although the olfactory membrane has 400 different receptors, we can actually detect*
    a. only 1,000 different odors.
    b. about 5,000 odors.
    c. about 10,000 odors.
    d. about 50,000 odors.

25. *The idea that chemicals in the nose produce odors when part of the odor molecule matches a receptor site of the same shape in the nose is called*
    a. lock and key theory.
    b. pheromone theory.
    c. sensory adaptation.
    d. sensory reception.

26. *Which of the following is NOT a taste quality?*
    a. sweet
    b. salty
    c. brothy
    d. spicy

27. *Which of the following is NOT considered a somesthetic sense?*
    a. skin senses
    b. kinesthetic senses
    c. vestibular senses
    d. olfactory senses

28. *Pain associated with the skin, muscles, joints, and tendons is called*
    a. visceral pain.
    b. referred pain.
    c. somatic pain.
    d. muscular pain.

29. *When a sensory message fails to reach awareness because it is altered in the spinal cord, this is known as*
    a. sensory adaptation.
    b. selective attention.
    c. sensory gating.
    d. subliminal perception.

30. *Sensory conflict theory is often used to explain*
    a. the relationship between smell and taste.
    b. sensory illusions.
    c. motion sickness.
    d. hallucinations.

31. *Connor cannot smell his own body odor but is noted to complain about the smell of others. What might explain this apparent discrepancy?*
    a. sensory adaptation
    b. olfactory refusal
    c. selective attention
    d. counterirritation

32. *Larry is red-green color-blind. This means*
    a. he can only differentiate between the colors red and green.
    b. Larry has a very rare type of color blindness.
    c. color interpretation is generally weak.
    d. he perceives the colors red and green as being the same.

33. *The danger of hearing loss depends on*
    a. the loudness.
    b. the length of time exposed to the sound.
    c. both a & b.
    d. none of the above

34. *Airborne chemicals, which are often used by animals to identify territory and even family members, are known as*
    a. VNO.
    b. exposure odors.
    c. pheromones.
    d. phonemes.

35. *Each of the following is a factor that can reduce pain EXCEPT*
    a. lowered levels of anxiety.
    b. increased attention to the source of pain.
    c. interpretation.
    d. counterirritation.

PERCEPTION

While a person may be flooded with sensory information, it is **perception** that actively assembles those sensations into a usable mental representation of the world around us.

E.R. Degginger/Animals Animals

Mark McKenna

Gestalt Principles

Gestalt psychologists concluded that several factors bring order to our perceptions.

Organizing Sensations

Attended sensations become part of the percept. To effectively use sensory input, a variety of organizational principles are used to form perceptions.

Vision

Our eyes make major contributions to our perceptual experience.

Constructing Perceptions

Perceptual construction occurs through **bottom-up and top-down processing**. Occurring simultaneously, bottom-up processing begins with small sensory units and builds up, while top-down processing applies preexisting knowledge to organize features into a meaningful whole.

Perceptual Accuracy

Perceptual sets influence what we perceive. The accuracy of perceptions can be improved through reality testing, dishabituation, conscious efforts to pay attention, and an awareness of factors that contribute to erroneous perceptions.

Perceptual Influences

Perception is imperfect. Such factors as learning, values, motives, expectations, and attention affect private perceptual experience. Eyewitnesses often are not reliable.

Misperception

Eyewitnesses frequently misperceive events—even important events such as crimes or accidents.

Abilities

ESP and other **psi phenomena** include the ability to perceive events or information in ways unaffected by distance (clairvoyance), the ability to read minds (telepathy), the ability to predict future events (precognition), and the ability to influence objects purely with the mind (psychokinesis).

EXTRASENSORY PERCEPTION (ESP)

Reported abilities to perceive events in ways that cannot be explained by known sensory capacities are known as **extrasensory perception.**

Evidence

Research in **parapsychology** remains controversial, owing to a variety of problems and shortcomings. The bulk of evidence is against ESP.

CHAPTER 5

Perceiving the World

Figure and Ground

The division of sensations into figure (object) and ground (background) is the most basic organizational principle.

After Leeper, 1935.

Perceptual Organization

Nearness, similarity, continuity, closure, contiguity, and common region of stimuli all contribute to the organization of sensations.

Constancies

Our vision would be unstable and would seem distorted and erratic if not for the perceptual constancies of size, shape, and brightness.

Depth Perception

We construct three-dimensional space through the use of **binocular and monocular depth** cues. Binocular cues include retinal disparity and convergence. Monocular cues include accommodation and pictoral cues of linear perspective, relative size, height in the picture plane, light and shadow, overlap, texture gradients, aerial haze, and motion parallax.

© 2006 "Pintos" by Bev Doolittle®, courtesy of The Greenwich Workshop, Inc. www.greenwichworkshop.com

Chapter Concepts

- *Perception is an active process of assembling sensations into meaningful patterns that represent external events.*
- *Size, shape, and brightness constancies bring stability to our vision, which would otherwise seem distorted and erratic.*
- *We unconsciously use Gestalt principles to organize sensations into meaningful patterns.*
- *Our wondrous ability to perceive three-dimensional space is largely based on retinal disparity (a difference between what the right and left eyes see).*
- *Depth perception also depends on bodily cues and pictorial cues that provide added information about depth and distance.*
- *Perception is greatly affected by learning, motives, values attention, and expectations. Private perceptual experiences don't always accurately represent external events.*
- *Eyewitnesses frequently misperceive events—even important events such as crimes or accidents.*
- *You can improve the accuracy and objectivity of your perceptions through conscious effort and an awareness of factors that contribute to erroneous perceptions.*
- *Scientific evidence concerning the existence of extrasensory perception is mostly negative or inconclusive.*

Concept Review

1. If you look at a book, rotating it several ways, you still perceive it as rectangular. This is called _____ constancy.
   a. size
   b. shape
   c. brightness
   d. rotational

2. Which Gestalt principle helps us see illusory figures?
   a. similarity
   b. continuity
   c. closure
   d. contiguity

3. Which Gestalt principle is the reason uniformed band members that are randomly scattered on a football field are perceived as a group instead of individuals?
   a. similarity
   b. continuity
   c. closure
   d. contiguity

4. Which Gestalt principle refers to perceiving causality in things that are near each other in time or space?
   a. similarity
   b. continuity
   c. closure
   d. contiguity

5. Although Devin is only 5 feet 5 inches tall, he seems tall when around the rest of his family, who only average a height of 4 feet 10 inches. This effect on perception is commonly referred to as
   a. an illusion.
   b. feedback.
   c. context.
   d. design.

6. Research into depth perception has shown that can begin to develop as early as
   a. 2 weeks of age.
   b. 2 months of age.
   c. 6 months of age.
   d. 1 year of age.

7. Which of the following is a binocular cue for depth?
   a. accommodation
   b. disconvergence
   c. retinal disparity
   d. retinal illumination

8. What occurs when two different images are fused into one overall image?
   a. accommodation
   b. convergence
   c. stereoscopic vision
   d. retinal illumination

9. Mountain ranges in the western United States often appear to be much closer than they really are. This is due to
   a. linear perspective.
   b. texture gradient.
   c. overlap.
   d. aerial perspective.

10. _____ is also known as interposition.
    a. Linear perspective
    b. Texture gradient
    c. Overlap
    d. Aerial perspective

11. Apparent-distance hypothesis explains the _____ illusion.
    a. Müller-Lyer
    b. moon
    c. size-distance
    d. linear

12. Changes in the brain that alter how we construct sensory information into percepts are called perceptual
    a. learning.
    b. habits.
    c. expectancy.
    d. set.

13. Which of the following refers to changes in perception that can be attributed to prior experience?
    a. learning
    b. habits
    c. expectancy
    d. set

14. In the inverted vision study,
    a. subjects were unable to adapt.
    b. the world always seemed abnormal.
    c. subjects suffered no physical ills.
    d. subjects were eventually able to perform most routine activities.

15. The difference between an illusion and a hallucination is that the latter
    a. is a distortion of stimuli that actually exist.
    b. is seen by other people as well.
    c. may have practical uses.
    d. is a perceived event with no external reality.

16. Gregory found that Zulus
    a. do not experience the Müller-Lyer illusion.
    b. perceive the world as we do.
    c. live in a world of straight lines.
    d. do not experience the moon illusion.

17. Vicki often talks on her cell phone while driving to and from work. Aside from being dangerous, this is also an example of
    a. selective attention.
    b. divided attention.
    c. attention without awareness.
    d. momentary lapse of consciousness.

18. Which is NOT one of the most basic sources of attention?
    a. habituation
    b. change
    c. contrast
    d. incongruity

19. If you are anticipating a starter pistol to fire, you tend to notice billboards of cars more than other advertisements. This illustrates the role of _____ in perception.
    a. vision
    b. motives
    c. contrast
    d. expectancy

20. When a student attempts to solve a new puzzle, she will most likely use
    a. top-down processing.
    b. bottom-up processing.
    c. perceptual expectancy.
    d. perceptual incongruity.

21. Once, when I was expecting an important phone call, the doorbell rang. I picked up the phone, a mistake no doubt caused by which of the following?
    a. top-down processing
    b. bottom-up processing
    c. perceptual expectancy
    d. perceptual incongruity

22. Eyewitness testimony
    a. is more accurate when the witness is confident.
    b. is nearly infallible.
    c. is nearly an "instant replay."
    d. is frequently wrong.

23. Which of the following could distort a person's perception of an event?
    a. being surprised
    b. being threatened
    c. being under stress
    d. all of the above

24. Jack is a victim to a crime and is asked to identify the culprit that pointed the gun to his head. Even though he stood two feet from the criminal he cannot remember anything about his face. This is an example of
    a. weapons focus.
    b. unconscious transference.
    c. accuracy confidence.
    d. exposure time.

25. Which of the following is NOT one of the seven ways to become a better eyewitness?
    a. Use perceptual habits.
    b. Beware of perceptual sets.
    c. Engage in reality testing.
    d. Pay attention.

26. Extrasensory perception of another person's thoughts is called
    a. clairvoyance.
    b. telepathy.
    c. precognition.
    d. psychokinesis.

27. The supposed ability to exert influence over inanimate objects is called
    a. clairvoyance.
    b. telepathy.
    c. precognition.
    d. psychokinesis.

28. From a set of 12 cards of the same suit, a person is able to predict the correct value of the card about 20% of the time. What can most likely account for this success rate?
    a. dishabituation
    b. run of luck
    c. ESP
    d. perceptual set

29. Modern parapsychologists, remembering the fraud perpetrated in the Rhine studies involving Zener cards, are careful to recognize the importance of
    a. double-blind experiments.
    b. security.
    c. accuracy in record keeping.
    d. All of the above.

30. This refers to the illusory motion perceived when objects are shown in rapidly changing positions.
    a. stereoscopic vision
    b. stroboscopic vision
    c. retinal disparity
    d. monocular vision

31. _____ is the process by which we assemble sensations into meaningful patterns.
    a. Sensation organization
    b. Perception
    c. Sensory illusion
    d. Perceptual refining

32. A television commercial that states the product's name repeatedly is attempting to gain you're attention through:
    a. product annoyance.
    b. contrasting stimulation.
    c. repetitious stimuli.
    d. product brain-washing.

33. Elizabeth has heard the faucet drip for the last week. Now she no longer notices the sound. This would be an example of
    a. confabulation.
    b. inhabituation.
    c. dishabituation.
    d. habituation.

34. What are you observing when you see a person stop to take a second look at something?
    a. orientation response
    b. stereoscopic vision
    c. the boiled-frog syndrome
    d. retinal disparity

35. Figure-ground organization is
    a. probably inborn.
    b. the first perceptual ability to appear after cataract patients regain sight.
    c. a Gestalt principle.
    d. all of the above

CONSCIOUSNESS

Consciousness consists of all the sensations, perceptions, memories, and feelings we are aware of at any instant. **Altered states of consciousness** involve changes in the quality and pattern of mental activity. Altered states may have important cultural meanings.

Courtesy of Maryanne Mott

Sleep

Sleep is necessary for survival of the individual. **Sleep deprivation** can lead to a variety of physical and mental deficits. Sleep patterns show some flexibility with 7 to 8 hours average.

Hypnosis

Hypnosis is characterized by narrowed attention and increased suggestibility. It can produce relaxation, control pain, and alter perceptions. It is more effective at changing subjective experiences than habits.

Meditation and Sensory Deprivation

Meditation is used to alter consciousness through the focusing of attention and interruption of the normal flow of thoughts. It is effective in producing the **relaxation response**, as can sensory deprivation.

Psychoactive Drugs

Americans regularly use consciousness-altering drugs. Psychoactive drugs directly influence brain activity. Most can be placed on a scale ranging from **stimulant** (upper) to **depressant** (downer).

REM and Non-REM Sleep

Sleep occurs in two basic states: rapid eye movement (REM) sleep and non-REM (NREM) sleep.

Sleep Disorders

Insomnia, the most common sleep disorder, may be temporary or chronic. Other disorders include sleepwalking, night terrors, narcolepsy, and sleep apnea, which may play a role in sudden infant death syndrome. Many of the disorders are serious health problems that should be corrected if they persist.

Dreams

Most dreams are about familiar things, and dream content is about equally positive and negative. Nightmares are dreams with negative emotional content. Dreams are as meaningful as waking thoughts. Debate remains about whether or not they have deeper, symbolic meaning, although interpretation of dreams can increase self-awareness.

Drug Abuse

Drug abuse has been one of the most persistent of all social problems in Western nations. Psychoactive drugs tend to create **drug dependence**, which may be physical (addiction) or psychological. **Addiction** occurs most with drugs that cause **withdrawal symptoms**, and addiction is often accompanied by **drug tolerance.**

Uppers

Drugs such as amphetamines, cocaine, MDMA, caffeine, and nicotine excite the central nervous system.

Downers

Drugs such as alcohol, tranquilizers, and sedatives depress central nervous system function. Alcohol is the most heavily abused drug in common use.

Hallucinogens

Marijuana, LSD, and PCP alter sensory impressions. Marijuana is the most popular illicit drug in America.

REM Sleep

REM sleep is strongly associated with dreaming. It aids the processing of memories and contributes to general mental effectiveness.

BSIP/Photo Researchers, Inc.

Non-REM Sleep

Non-REM sleep occurs in four stages, ranging from shallow to deep. Each stage is marked by different brain wave patterns, as measured by **electroencephalograph.**

Expuesto-Nicolas Randall/Alamy

Patterns of Abuse

Drug-taking behavior may be experimental, recreational, situational, intensive, or compulsive. Drug abuse is most often associated with the last three.

CHAPTER 6

States of Consciousness

Corbis/SuperStock

Chapter Concepts

- *Consciousness and altered states of awareness are core features of mental life.*
- *Sleep is necessary for survival. It occurs in four stages from shallow to deep and in two basic states, REM sleep and non-REM sleep.*
- *Sleep loss and sleep disorders are serious health problems that should be corrected when they persist.*
- *REM sleep helps us form memories, and it contributes to general mental effectiveness.*
- *Dreams are at least as meaningful as waking thoughts. Whether they have deeper, symbolic meaning is still debated.*
- *Collecting and interpreting your dreams can promote self-awareness.*
- *Hypnosis is useful but not "magical." Hypnosis can change private experiences more readily than behaviors or habits.*
- *Psychoactive drugs, which alter consciousness, are highly prone to abuse.*
- *Drug abuse is related to personal maladjustment, the reinforcing qualities of drugs, peer group influences, and expectations about drug effects.*

Concept Review

1. *A state of clear, organized alertness is*
   a. consciousness.
   b. waking consciousness.
   c. altered state of consciousness.
   d. mania.

2. *Which of the following might cause an altered state of consciousness?*
   a. sleep
   b. drug use
   c. sensory overload
   d. all of the above

3. *After being awake for more than 60 hours, a person may develop hallucinations and delusional thinking in a state called*
   a. microsleep syndrome.
   b. sleep deprivation.
   c. sleep deprivation psychosis.
   d. abnormal awareness.

4. *Persons over age 50 generally average about _____ hours of sleep per night.*
   a. 6
   b. 8
   c. 9
   d. 10

5. *In which of the stages of sleep would a person be most difficult to wake?*
   a. Stage 1
   b. Stage 2
   c. Stage 3
   d. Stage 4

6. *In which stage do sleep spindles appear on the EEG?*
   a. Stage 1
   b. Stage 2
   c. Stage 3
   d. Stage 4

7. *In which stage would a hypnic jerk be most likely to occur?*
   a. Stage 1
   b. Stage 2
   c. Stage 3
   d. Stage 4

8. *The bulk of our dreaming is done during*
   a. Stage 4, deep sleep.
   b. NREM sleep.
   c. REM sleep.
   d. Stage 2, light sleep.

9. *During which type of sleep are muscles paralyzed?*
   a. Stage 4, deep sleep
   b. NREM sleep
   c. REM sleep
   d. Stage 2, light sleep

10. *Which of the following is true of NREM sleep?*
    a. It may help the body recover from bodily fatigue.
    b. Breathing becomes irregular.
    c. NREM sleep is marked by fast EEG patterns.
    d. Dreams are more vivid and emotional during NREM.

11. *When do night terrors and sleepwalking occur?*
    a. Stage 4, deep sleep
    b. NREM sleep
    c. REM sleep
    d. Stage 2, light sleep

12. *During which type of sleep would nightmares typically occur?*
    a. Stage 4, deep sleep
    b. NREM sleep
    c. REM sleep
    d. Stage 2, light sleep

13. *All of the following are reasonable treatments for insomnia EXCEPT*
    a. exercise.
    b. sleep restriction.
    c. relaxation.
    d. caffeine consumption.

14. *Which of the following is NOT likely to occur during NREM sleep?*
    a. nightmares
    b. night terrors
    c. sleepwalking
    d. sleeptalking

15. *A hereditary problem in which the victim has irresistible "sleep attacks" in the day is called*
    a. REM behavior disorder.
    b. narcolepsy.
    c. sleep apnea.
    d. excessive daytime sleepiness.

16. *Sleep apnea refers to a problem with*
    a. falling asleep.
    b. breathing during sleep.
    c. falling directly into REM sleep.
    d. staying asleep.

17. *The idea that dreams contain hidden, symbolic meaning was first proposed by*
    a. Hall.
    b. Freud.
    c. Hobson.
    d. McCarley.

18. *The theory that dreaming is just the brain's way of explaining its own physical activity is called*
    a. wish fulfillment.
    b. activation synthesis.
    c. secondary elaboration.
    d. condensation.

19. *Which of the following is NOT a characteristic of hypnosis?*
    a. narrowed attention
    b. increased suggestibility
    c. altered state of consciousness
    d. sleep state

20. *Evidence shows that hypnosis does not produce*
    a. sensory changes.
    b. amnesia.
    c. superhuman acts of strength.
    d. pain relief.

21. *Scientists have found that mild sensory deprivation can do all but which of the following?*
    a. increase intelligence
    b. help people lose weight
    c. help people quit smoking
    d. reduce alcohol use

22. *Stimulants _____ nervous system activity, whereas depressants _____ it.*
    a. reduce; enhance
    b. enhance; increase
    c. increase; decrease
    d. reduce; decrease

23. *Which term refers to the increasing need for greater amounts of a drug to produce the same effect?*
    a. physical addiction
    b. psychological addiction
    c. drug tolerance
    d. withdrawal

24. *The pattern of drug use in which drugs are used to cope with a specific problem, such as staying awake, is called*
    a. experimental.
    b. social-recreational.
    c. situational.
    d. compulsive.

25. *Which stimulant is synthetically produced?*
    a. amphetamines
    b. cocaine
    c. caffeine
    d. nicotine

26. *Which of the following is a withdrawal symptom associated with cocaine?*
    a. anhedonia
    b. lowered anxiety
    c. fatigue
    d. boredom

27. *The single most preventable cause of death in the United States and Canada is*
    a. smoking.
    b. cocaine.
    c. heroin.
    d. barbiturates.

28. *_____ refers to drinking five or more drinks in a short time.*
    a. Initial abuse phase
    b. Detoxification
    c. Chronic drinking
    d. Binge-drinking

29. *Which drug is actually an anesthetic?*
    a. LSD
    b. mescaline
    c. psilocybin
    d. PCP

30. *At high dosages, marijuana can cause*
    a. paranoia.
    b. hallucinations.
    c. delusions.
    d. all of the above

31. *Health risks of marijuana use include all but which of the following?*
    a. higher levels of activation within the cerebellum
    b. lowered sperm production
    c. increased risk of a variety of cancers
    d. suppression of the immune system

32. *With regard to Freud's four dream processes, the tendency to make a dream more logical and add details to it when remembering it is called*
    a. condensation.
    b. displacement.
    c. symbolization.
    d. secondary elaboration.

33. *Which of the following is not a step described by the text for use in avoiding the continuation of a bad dream?*
    a. Write down the dream.
    b. Imagery rehearsal.
    c. Change the details of the dream, making a more pleasant dream.
    d. Try to immediately fall back to sleep.

34. *Sleep apnea is suspected as a possible contributing cause for the occurrence of _____.*
    a. cataplexy
    b. SIDS
    c. narcolepsy
    d. REM rebound

35. *Jacob reported that during one of his dreams last night, he knew he was dreaming. This would be an example of a _____ dream.*
    a. latent
    b. lucid
    c. manifest
    d. conscious

LEARNING

Learning is a relatively permanent change in behavior due to experience. Learning principles can be used to understand and manage behavior.

Associative Learning

Associative learning is a simple type of learning in which associations are made between stimuli and responses. Classical and operant conditioning are two types of associative learning that affect many aspects of life.

Classical Conditioning

In this form of learning, an **antecedent** stimulus that doesn't naturally produce a response is linked with a stimulus that does. When that neutral stimulus comes to elicit the response, learning has occurred.

Carleton Ray/Photo Researchers, Inc.

Observational Learning (Modeling)

Observation of models influences behavior. The personal characteristics of the model and the success or failure of their behavior influences whether their behavior will be replicated. Media characters can be powerful models for this type of learning.

Albert Bandura/Stanford University

Operant Conditioning

In this form of learning, the **consequences** of the response determine if the behavior will be voluntarily repeated. When the response has changed due to reinforcement or punishment, learning has occurred.

Chimp-O-Mat, Yerkes Regional Primate Research Center, Emory University

Cognitive Learning

Cognitive learning involves higher mental processes. Both animals and people seem to form **cognitive maps. Latent learning** is that which remains unseen until reward for performance is offered. **Discovery learning** emphasizes insight and understanding.

CHAPTER 7

Conditioning and Learning

Stimuli and Responses

An **unconditioned stimulus (US)** is a stimulus that reliably provokes an **unconditioned response (UR)**. When the **neutral stimulus (NS)** begins to produce the response, then the response becomes a **conditioned response (CR)**. The neutral stimulus, no longer neutral, becomes a **conditioned stimulus (CS)**.

Christoph Wilhelm/Getty Images

Strengthening and Weakening Responses

Conditioning is strengthened when the CS is followed by the US. It is extinguished when the CS is presented alone. In **higher-order conditioning**, a well-learned CS is used like a US to induce further learning.

Recovering Memories

Although memories of trauma and abuse may be repressed, there is significant debate over recovered memories of childhood sexual abuse. When there is no other evidence of such, extreme caution is warrented.

Dan Barba/Jupiterimages

Chapter Concepts

- *Conditioning is a fundamental type of learning that affects many aspects of daily life.*
- *In classical conditioning, a neutral stimulus is repeatedly paired with a stimulus that reliably provokes a response. By association, the neutral stimulus also begins to elicit a response.*
- *In operant conditioning, responses that are followed by reinforcement occur more frequently.*
- *To understand why people behave as they do, it is important to identify how their responses are being reinforced.*
- *Cognitive learning involves acquiring higher-level information, rather than just linking stimuli and responses.*
- *We also learn by observing and imitating the actions of others.*
- *Behavioral principles can be used to manage one's own behavior.*

Shaping Behavior

When the desired response is not present, behavior can be shaped (gradually molded) into a desired pattern by using **successive approximations**.

Bambu Productions/Getty Images

Reinforcement

Positive and negative reinforcement increase the likelihood of responses being repeated.

Primary and Secondary Reinforcers

Primary reinforcers are directly reinforcing, as they fulfill biological needs. Secondary reinforcers lead to primary reinforcers.

Punishment

Responses that are followed by punishment become less frequent. Punishment tends to produce **escape learning** and **avoidance learning**.

Schedules of Reinforcement

Reinforcement may be given continuously or on a partial schedule. Partial reinforcement schedules may be based on occurrences of behavior **(ratio)** or on time periods **(interval)** and may be **fixed** or **variable**.

Concept Review

1. *Learning is defined as*
   a. relatively permanent.
   b. a change in behavior.
   c. due to experience.
   d. all of the above

2. *In classical conditioning, _____ are important, while in operant conditioning, _____ are primary for learning.*
   a. antecedents; consequences
   b. consequences; antecedents
   c. responses; reflexes
   d. responses; antecedents

3. *When a tone is sounded, a infant's right cheek is touched, and the baby reflexively turns its head to the direction of the touch. After several pairings, the baby turns its head to the right as soon as it hears the tone. In this example, the conditioned stimulus is the*
   a. touch.
   b. tone.
   c. head turning.
   d. eye movement.

4. *In the example described in Question 3, which answer choice is the unconditioned stimulus?*
   a. touch
   b. tone
   c. head turning
   d. eye movement

5. *In the example described in Question 3, if a clicking noise were made just before the tone is sounded, the baby would eventually turn its head to the clicking noise as well. This is known as*
   a. shaping.
   b. stimulus generalization.
   c. higher-order conditioning.
   d. spontaneous recovery.

6. *If the baby in this example were to hear a tone similar to the original one and turn its head, we could say that*
   a. shaping has occurred.
   b. stimulus generalization has occurred.
   c. higher-order conditioning has occurred.
   d. spontaneous recovery has occurred.

7. *If the same baby was to continue to hear the tone, but the touch did not follow the repeated tones, what would eventually be likely to occur?*
   a. Nothing; learning is permanent.
   b. The baby would cry.
   c. The baby would continue to turn.
   d. The baby would stop turning his or her head.

8. *Chris used to love dogs but was badly bitten by a stray dog once. Now he is extremely fearful when he sees any dog nearing him. This is an example of*
   a. a conditioned emotional response.
   b. an anxiety disorder.
   c. an operant.
   d. systematic desensitization.

9. *Karen and her husband are very prejudiced. Their daughter Nikki, although only a small child, also reacts very negatively to people who are different from her. Her emotional response is most likely due to*
   a. shaping.
   b. vicarious conditioning.
   c. stimulus generalization.
   d. stimulus discrimination.

10. *Like classical conditioning, operant conditioning is*
    a. based on information and expectancies.
    b. based on reflexive responses.
    c. based on antecedent stimuli.
    d. based on consistent consequences.

11. *First, Rover is rewarded for walking through a hoop when the hoop is on the ground. Then the hoop is raised a little, and Rover is rewarded again for stepping through. If this is repeated until Rover is jumping through the hoop, _____ has occurred.*
    a. stimulus generalization
    b. stimulus discrimination
    c. extinction
    d. shaping

12. *_____ is the ability to respond differently to various stimuli.*
    a. Extinction
    b. Discrimination
    c. Negative reinforcement
    d. Spontaneous recovery

13. *If parents ignore a child's temper tantrums and the tantrums subsequently cease, _____ has occurred.*
    a. stimulus generalization
    b. stimulus discrimination
    c. operant extinction
    d. shaping

14. *George has learned that if he gives in to his son Brandon and lets Brandon have the toy he is screaming for in the store, the screaming stops. George continues giving in because of his own*
    a. positive reinforcement.
    b. negative reinforcement.
    c. punishment.
    d. response cost punishment.

15. *George finally tells Brandon that not only will he NOT get a toy when he screams for it, but he will also have one of the toys he already has taken away from him if he does scream. George is using*
    a. positive reinforcement.
    b. negative reinforcement.
    c. positive punishment.
    d. negative punishment.

16. *Which of these is an example of a primary reinforcer?*
    a. getting a gold star for being good
    b. receiving a paycheck
    c. giving a child a hug
    d. giving a child a token

17. *Which is NOT one of the three factors increasing the effectiveness of feedback?*
    a. frequent
    b. immediate
    c. detailed
    d. positive

18. *Continuously reinforced responses are*
    a. based on real-life reinforcement.
    b. hard to eliminate.
    c. useless in the laboratory.
    d. easy to extinguish.

19. *Mitch is selling magazine subscriptions. For every five subscriptions he sells, he gets one dollar. This exemplifies*
    a. a fixed-ratio schedule.
    b. a variable-ratio schedule.
    c. a fixed-interval schedule.
    d. a variable-interval schedule.

20. *Gambling is related to which of the following?*
    a. fixed-ratio schedule
    b. variable-ratio schedule
    c. fixed-interval schedule
    d. variable-interval schedule

21. *Fishing operates on which reinforcement schedule?*
    a. fixed-ratio schedule
    b. variable-ratio schedule
    c. fixed-interval schedule
    d. variable-interval schedule

22. *Seeing a vehicle with colored lights mounted to its roof may cause a driver to alter their driving. What term best describes this process?*
    a. discriminative stimulus
    b. reinforcement
    c. negative punishment
    d. negative stimulus

23. *Which of these statements about punishment is FALSE?*
    a. It needs to be immediate.
    b. It is long-lasting.
    c. It needs to be applied consistently to the undesired behavior.
    d. It works better when paired with reinforcement of the desired response.

24. *Upon returning home from work, David punishes his puppy (by placing the dog in a "time-out" box for several minutes). Which rule of punishment has David broken?*
    a. It needs to be immediate.
    b. It is long-lasting.
    c. It needs to be consistent.
    d. It works best if it is severe.

25. *Jean sometimes spanks her son for getting out of bed at night to play, but many times she just decides not to put him back to bed. Which rule of punishment is she disregarding?*
    a. It needs to be immediate.
    b. It uses counter conditioning.
    c. It needs to be consistent.
    d. It works better when paired with reinforcement of the desired response.

26. *Punishment can*
    a. create fear of the punisher.
    b. result in escape learning, such as lying.
    c. can greatly increase aggression.
    d. all of the above

27. *Understanding, anticipating, and knowing are parts of*
    a. cognitive learning.
    b. mental learning.
    c. response learning.
    d. knowledge learning.

28. *Skills gained by insight are an example of*
    a. cognitive maps.
    b. latent learning.
    c. discovery learning.
    d. observational learning.

29. *Which of the following refers to a mental representation of an external area?*
    a. cognitive map
    b. latent learning
    c. discovery learning
    d. observational learning

30. *Which of the following is an example of latent learning?*
    a. A student displays math knowledge only when having the incentive to get a good grade on a test.
    b. A student learns how to solve a math problem through sudden insight.
    c. A student displays math knowledge only when in danger of getting a poor test grade.
    d. A student displays math knowledge by solving a problem through trial and error.

31. *Carrie wants to be a gymnast. Unfortunately, she weighs 200 pounds and is 6 foot 4 inches tall. Which of the following will prevent her from learning through observation?*
    a. paying attention
    b. remembering what was done
    c. reproducing what was done
    d. being motivated to learn

32. *Televised violence*
    a. causes all children to become more aggressive.
    b. hinders aggression later in life.
    c. may increase the likelihood of children to behave aggressively.
    d. none of the above

33. *Operant conditioning is to _____ as classical conditioning is to _____.*
    a. voluntary behavior; reflexive behavior
    b. learning; behavior
    c. antecedents; consequences
    d. trial; effect

34. *Which of the following is not one of the four strategies identified by your text for helping change bad habits?*
    a. Alternate responses
    b. Extinction
    c. Response chains
    d. Cognitive contracting

35. *_____ appear to produce reinforcement, even though actually being unnecessary.*
    a. Response chains
    b. Superstitious behaviors
    c. Positive behaviors
    d. Vicarious behaviors

MEMORY

Memory is an active process in which information is received, organized, altered, stored, and recovered. Information coming into memory must be **encoded**, **stored**, and **retrieved**.

Sensory, Short-Term, and Long-Term Memory

Humans appear to have three types of inter-related memory systems. Different strategies are required to make the best use of the memory systems.

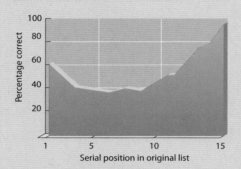

Sensory Memory

Sensory organs collect information that is retained for a short period of time. Sensory memories are encoded as **iconic** or **echoic** memories.

Encoding Failure

Often, memory failures occur because information wasn't stored in the first place.

Forgetting

Failure to encode, store, or retrieve can all be the source of forgetting. Forgetting is most rapid immediately after learning.

William Fritsch/Jupiterimages

Interference

New learning can interfere with the ability to retrieve earlier learning **(retroactive interference)**, and old learning can interfere with the retrieval of new learning **(proactive interference)**.

Improving Memory

The quality of memory varies from individual to individual. Some people are more skilled at retrieving information than others. A small number of people have **eidetic imagery**. Everyone can learn new memory skills.

Memory Systems

Mnemonics greatly improve immediate memory. When studying or memorizing, keep in mind the effects of serial position, sleep, review, cues, and elaboration.

CHAPTER 8

Memory

Richard Heinzen/SuperStock

Short-Term Memory (STM)

STM is a temporary storehouse for small amounts of information. STM's limited capacity can be enhanced with **chunking** and **maintenance rehearsal**.

Long-Term Memory (LTM)

LTM is a large storehouse for meaningful information with basically unlimited capacity. With **elaborative encoding**, longer lasting memories are formed. LTM contains **procedural** and **declarative memories**; the latter may be **semantic** or **episodic**.

Decay

Forgetting in sensory memory and STM can be caused by storage failure through decaying **memory traces**. Decay may also explain some LTM losses in the case of disuse.

Cue Dependency

Some memories rely on cues in the environment for successful retrieval. **State-dependent learning** is an example.

Psychological Motives

Repression (unconscious) or **suppression** (conscious) of memories may occur for psychological reasons.

Recovered Memories

Although memories of trauma and abuse may be repressed, there is significant debate over recovered memories of childhood sexual abuse. When there is no other evidence of such, extreme caution is warranted.

AP/Wide World Photo

Chapter Concepts

- *Remembering is an active process. Memories are often lost, altered, revised, or distorted.*
- *Different strategies are required to make the best use of short-term memory and long-term memory.*
- *Remembering is not an all-or-nothing process. Information that appears to be lost may still reside in memory.*
- *An inability to retrieve information isn't the only cause of forgetting. Often, memory failures occur because information wasn't stored in the first place.*
- *Extreme caution is warranted when "recovered" memories are the only basis for believing that a person was sexually abused during childhood.*
- *Although it's true that some people have naturally superior memories, everyone can learn to improve his or her memory.*
- *Memory systems (mnemonics) greatly improve immediate memory. However, conventional learning tends to create the most lasting memories.*

Concept Review

1. Sensory information is changed into a usable form to enter short-term memory in the process of
   a. memory.
   b. encoding.
   c. storage.
   d. retrieval.

2. A fleeting visual image that remains for about half a second after the original stimulus is gone is an
   a. icon.
   b. echo.
   c. imago.
   d. illusion.

3. Information is transferred from sensory memory to _____ by means of _____.
   a. short-term memory; rehearsal
   b. long-term memory; selective attention
   c. short-term memory; selective attention
   d. long-term memory; rehearsal

4. Which statement about short-term memory is FALSE?
   a. It is often encoded phonetically.
   b. It holds approximately seven bits of information (plus or minus two).
   c. It is also called working memory.
   d. It is not sensitive to interference.

5. Which statement about long-term memory is TRUE?
   a. It is relatively permanent.
   b. It is encoded visually.
   c. It has a finite capacity.
   d. Both a and c are true.

6. Remembering that "maison" sounds like "mason" and masons build houses, concluding the word "maison" means "house" in French is an example of
   a. maintenance rehearsal.
   b. elaborative encoding.
   c. chunking.
   d. recoding.

7. Loftus and Palmer have shown that memories are
   a. usually accurate.
   b. rarely altered.
   c. long lasting.
   d. at times updated, changed, or revised.

8. The network model of memory is supported by the phenomenon of _____ memory.
   a. redintegrative
   b. procedural
   c. declarative
   d. explicit

9. Which of the following refers to memories for skills such as tying your shoe laces?
   a. redintegrative
   b. procedural
   c. declarative
   d. explicit

10. The old biographical show "This Is Your Life" most likely utilized _____ memory, whereas "Jeopardy" uses _____ memory.
    a. procedural; declarative
    b. declarative; procedural
    c. episodic; semantic
    d. semantic; episodic

11. Multiple-choice tests utilize which kind of memory retrieval?
    a. recall
    b. recognition
    c. relearning
    d. revision

12. An essay test would require which type of retrieval?
    a. recall
    b. recognition
    c. relearning
    d. revision

13. An elderly man, suffering from mild dementia, insists that he does not know how to use his TV remote (even though he has had it a long time). When told to "just push a button," he pushes the correct buttons to turn the TV on and change the channels. His memory for the skill of using the remote has become
    a. explicit.
    b. implicit.
    c. unlearned.
    d. none of the above

14. A person who was exposed to the word "same" 2 hours earlier is more likely to complete the word fragment SA__ with the word "same." This is an example of
    a. exceptional memory.
    b. priming.
    c. relearning.
    d. explicit memory.

15. The text refers to _____ as typically being the most sensitive measure of memory.
    a. recognition
    b. serial position
    c. recall
    d. relearning

16. Ebbinghaus found that forgetting nonsense syllables was greatest
    a. after several days.
    b. after several weeks.
    c. shortly after learning.
    d. after many years.

17. Forgetting because we never really formed the memory in the first place is termed
    a. encoding failure.
    b. memory-trace decay.
    c. interference.
    d. repression.

18. The fading of memories is also referred to as
    a. encoding failure
    b. memory decay
    c. interference
    d. repression

19. *Sometimes you have to go back to the room in which you started to remember why you left it in the first place. This best illustrates*
    a. proactive interference.
    b. retroactive interference.
    c. cue-dependent memory.
    d. state-dependent memory.

20. *Bill has to put his car in the shop and get a rental car for a few days. His own car has the shift lever on the floor, but the rental has one on the wheel. When he first gets in the rental, he claws futilely at the floor. This illustrates which of the following concepts?*
    a. proactive interference
    b. retroactive interference
    c. cue-dependent memory
    d. state-dependent memory

21. *Allison can remember her current phone number but has forgotten the phone number at her last residence. This is considered an example of*
    a. proactive interference.
    b. retroactive interference.
    c. cue-dependent memory.
    d. state-dependent memory.

22. *Learning to stand aids a child with later learning how to walk. This is an example of*
    a. positive transfer.
    b. negative transfer.
    c. interference.
    d. repression.

23. *Which of the following is FALSE concerning flashbulb memories?*
    a. They are very detailed.
    b. They occur after an emotionally significant event.
    c. They are usually accurate.
    d. People place great confidence in the accuracy of their flashbulb memories.

24. *Sandy visited her cousin Sharon in the psychiatric ward. After the visit, Sharon received an electroconvulsive shock (ECS) treatment for her severe depression. On the next visit, Sandy was surprised to find that Sharon remembered nothing of the previous visit. This is because the ECS*
    a. frightened Sharon into repressing.
    b. worsened the depression.
    c. interfered with consolidation.
    d. altered Sharon's attention system.

25. *What part of the brain seems responsible for the formation of permanent memories?*
    a. amygdala
    b. hypothalamus
    c. cerebellum
    d. hippocampus

26. *Learning alters the _____ of brain cells.*
    a. activity
    b. structure
    c. chemistry
    d. all of the above

27. *If your textbook looks like it is "bleeding" yellow highlighter, you have probably violated which of the following methods for improving memory?*
    a. recitation
    b. organization
    c. selection
    d. overlearning

28. *While at a party, you are introduced to a large number of people. Later, you find you can only remember the names of the first few people and the last person you met. This illustrates the _____ effect.*
    a. state-dependent learning
    b. selection
    c. serial position
    d. spaced practice

29. *Which of the following is NOT good advice for improving memory?*
    a. Overlearn the material.
    b. Get a good night's sleep.
    c. Space out your practice sessions.
    d. Eat sparingly to maintain your "edge."

30. *Which of the following is NOT a step in the cognitive interview process?*
    a. Say or write down everything that relates to the information.
    b. Try to recall events only in the correct order.
    c. Recall from different viewpoints.
    d. Mentally re-create the situation.

31. *Any type of memory system or aid is known as*
    a. a memory method.
    b. forming a chain.
    c. a mnemonic.
    d. a recall system.

32. *If you experience the belief that you know a person's name but that it is not quite retrievable, you may be in a _____ state.*
    a. tip-of-the-tongue
    b. false memory
    c. serial position
    d. semantic

33. *Elizabeth is trying to forget the fatal car accident she witnessed two days ago. This attempt would be referred to as memory*
    a. decay.
    b. repression.
    c. suppression.
    d. none of the above

34. *_____ amnesia involves forgetting the events that followed an injury or trauma.*
    a. Partial
    b. Retroactive
    c. Retrograde
    d. Anterograde

35. *Eidetic imagery*
    a. is retained for at least 30 seconds.
    b. is "projected" onto a blank surface.
    c. is an ability more commonly found in children.
    d. all of the above

COGNITION, LANGUAGE, CREATIVITY, AND INTELLIGENCE

Thinking, language, problem solving and creativity are essential elements of being human. They underlie intelligent behavior. Mental abilities cover a wide range, and measuring these abilities can be challenging.

Cognition

Thinking (cognition) is influenced by how the information is mentally represented, which can come in the form of images, concepts, and language (symbols). Knowing the pitfalls of intuitive thought can aid in avoiding some common thinking errors.

Images and Concepts

Images are mental representations that can be three-dimensional or kinesthetic. Concepts are generalized ideas of classes of objects or events; they often make use of prototypes and may be **conjunctive** or **disjunctive**.

Problem Solving

The solution to a problem may be arrived at in a variety of ways. **Mechanical solutions** (such as trial and error) are often not efficient. **Heuristics** aid problem solving by narrowing the number of possible solutions. Deep comprehension, or **understanding**, is necessary for some problem solving. **Insight**, rapid solution resulting from understanding, can be blocked by fixations.

Divergent Thinking

Divergent thinking is characterized by fluency, flexibility, and originality. Tests of creativity measure these characteristics.

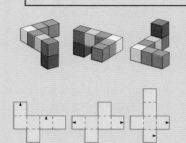

Creativity

To be creative, a solution must be practical and sensible as well as original. Creative thinking often occurs in five stages, and creative solutions often diverge from the norm.

Defining and Measuring Intelligence

Intelligence is operationally defined by intelligence tests that express intelligence in the form of an intelligence quotient **(IQ)**. These tests provide a useful but narrow estimate of real-world intelligence and are not universally valid for all cultural groups.

Intelligence

Intelligence is the overall capacity to think rationally, act purposefully, and deal effectively with the environment. It reflects combined effects of heredity and environment. Schooling and stimulating environments can induce changes in tested intelligence.

Range of Mental Abilities

The distribution of IQ scores follows a normal curve, with most people scoring in the mid-range. A very small percentage of people have exceptionally high or low IQ scores.

Adapted from Terman & Merrill, 1960.

Percent

24
20
16
12
8
4

Average
Bright normal
Dull normal
Superior
Borderline
Retarded
Very superior

40 60 80 100 120 140 160 180

Mean = 101.8   IQ

Language

Language is a system for encoding and manipulating information. Language carries meaning by combining symbols according to rules **(grammar)**, including rules about word order **(syntax)**. Meaning influences thinking in language.

The Great Ape Trust of Iowa

Creativity, Personality, and Intelligence

Research has identified characteristics of the creative personality. There is only a small correlation between creativity and IQ, and some creative skills can be learned.

Real-World Intelligence

Intelligence in the real world involves having some combination of a fast nervous system, learned knowledge, and an ability to manage how one thinks and solves problems. Many psychologists have begun to define and investigate intelligence in a broader way.

Getty Images

High IQ

High IQ and achievement have a strong correlation. High IQ (often labeled **gifted** or genius) reveals potential, but it does not guarantee success.

Intellectually Disabled

People with **intellectual disability** typically have low IQ or lack various adaptive behaviors. The majority can master basic adaptive behaviors and, with support, can find a place in the community.

CHAPTER 9

Cognition, Language, Creativity, and Intelligence

Manahem Kahana/AFP/Getty Images

Chapter Concepts

- *Thinking is influenced by the manner in which information is represented—as images, concepts, or symbols.*
- *Language is an especially powerful way to encode information and manipulate ideas.*
- *Animals are capable of rudimentary language use, but only with the aid of human intervention. Language is primarily a human characteristic.*
- *Expert problem solving is based on acquired knowledge and strategies. Experts are not naturally smarter than novices.*
- *Creative thinking is novel, divergent, and tempered with a dash of practicality.*
- *Some common thinking errors can be avoided if you know the pitfalls of intuitive thought.*
- *Creativity can be enhanced by strategies that promote divergent thinking.*
- *Intelligence tests provide a useful but narrow estimate of real-world intelligence.*
- *Everyone has special aptitudes (talents and potentials). Those who possess a wide range of mental abilities are above average in intelligence.*
- *Most people score in the mid-range on intelligence tests. Only a small percentage of people have exceptionally high and low IQ scores.*
- *A high IQ does not automatically lead to high achievement. A high IQ reveals potential, but it does not guarantee success.*
- *Both heredity and environment influence intelligence, but only improved social conditions and education (environment) can raise intelligence.*
- *Real-world intelligence combines a fast nervous system with learned knowledge and skills and an acquired ability to manage one's own thinking and problem solving.*
- *Traditional IQ tests measure linguistic, logical-mathematical, and spatial abilities. It is likely that we all use other types of intelligence in daily life.*
- *Traditional IQ tests are not universally valid for all cultural groups.*

Concept Review

1. Which is NOT one of the three basic units of thought?
   a. image
   b. prototype
   c. concept
   d. language

2. The WAIS-II divides intelligence into which of the following two IQ scores?
   a. performance and verbal intelligence
   b. emotional and verbal intelligence
   c. mathematical and verbal intelligence
   d. practical and common intelligence

3. IQ tests show a pattern of distribution called a
   a. bimodal distribution.
   b. normal (bell-shaped) curve.
   c. U-shaped curve.
   d. skewed curve.

4. Alex sees his first duck and learns to call it by the name "duck." Then he sees a chicken and calls it a duck, only to be corrected by his mother. The chicken would be an example of what in concept formation?
   a. positive instance
   b. negative instance
   d. conceptual rule
   d. prototype

5. Concepts that are defined by the presence of two or more features are called
   a. conjunctive.
   b. relational.
   c. disjunctive.
   d. prototypical.

6. Which of the following refers to concepts such as "larger," "above," and "left"?
   a. conjunctive
   b. relational
   c disjunctive
   d. prototypical

7. Which describes a concept that is the ideal example of the concept?
   a. conjunctive
   b. relational
   c. disjunctive
   d. prototypical

8. When MRI (magnetic resonance imaging) was first introduced as a brain-scanning technique, it was called NMRI (nuclear magnetic resonance imaging). The first word, nuclear, was dropped because people related the world nuclear to becoming radioactive. The change in names was to improve the _____ meaning of the term.
   a. semantic differential
   b. social
   c. denotative
   d. connotative

9. Which term is actually a way of measuring the connotative meaning of a word?
   a. semantic differential
   b. social
   c. denotative
   d. connotative

10. Which of the following is NOT considered faulty conceptualization?
    a. social stereotyping
    b. all-or-nothing thinking
    c. prototypical thinking
    d. All of the above are faulty.

11. Glenna felt like she was hit with a bolt of lightning when she solved the story problem. She wondered how she had not seen the answer sooner. This ability to reorganize and solve the problem quickly is an example of
    a. insight.
    b. understanding.
    c. perception.
    d. intuition.

12. Which type of bilingualism is undesirable for minority children?
    a. additive
    b. subtractive
    c. two-way
    d. interactive

13. Which aspect of language is violated by the English sentence, "I to school go."?
    a. transformation rules
    b. productivity
    c. syntax
    d. semantics

14. Which term is the set of rules for making sounds into words and words into sentences?
    a. transformation rules
    b. productivity
    c. grammar
    d. syntax

15. ASL
    a. is a true language.
    b. stands for American Sign Language.
    c. is a gestural language.
    d. all of the above

16. Which statement about experiments in teaching animals to talk is TRUE?
    a. Early attempts were very successful.
    b. Chimps have been taught to use sign language through operant conditioning.
    c. Washoe had a vocabulary of more than 1,000 signs.
    d. Chimps cannot use conditional sentences to communicate with humans.

17. Trial-and-error learning is an example of
    a. a mechanical solution.
    b. solutions by understanding.
    c. an insightful solution.
    d. a general solution.

18. If the number of alternatives for solving a problem is small, a(n) _____ may work best.
    a. heuristic
    b. functional solution
    c. random search strategy
    d. insightful solution

19. *Which term refers to a strategy that is a "rule of thumb"?*
   a. heuristic
   b. functional solution
   c. random search strategy
   d. insightful solution

20. *Bringing together seemingly unrelated bits of useful information is called*
   a. selective comparison.
   b. selective combination.
   c. selective encoding.
   d. functional fixedness.

21. *Which common barrier to problem solving includes functional fixedness?*
   a. emotional barriers
   b. cultural barriers
   d. learned barriers
   d. perceptual barriers

22. *One of the differences between experts and novices in a particular field is*
   a. experts use more trial-and-error thinking.
   b. novices rely more heavily on acquired strategies than experts.
   c. experts can recognize patterns in material more easily.
   d. novices engage in more automatic problem solving than experts.

23. *Thought that goes from general principles to specific situations is called _____ thought.*
   a. inductive
   b. deductive
   c. logical
   d. illogical

24. *In creative thinking, _____ is the total number of suggestions you are able to make.*
   a. fluency
   b. flexibility
   c. originality
   d. automaticity

25. *Multiple-choice items on an exam most probably measure*
   a. divergent thinking.
   b. convergent thinking.
   c. flexibility.
   d. originality.

26. *Howard Gardner has proposed that there are actually _____ different kinds of intelligence.*
   a. three
   b. five
   c. eight
   d. 12

27. *Mental retardation is diagnosed by IQs*
   a. approximately 70 or below.
   b. below 55.
   c. between 20 and 40.
   d. at or below 85.

28. *Which of the following is the correct sequence in creative thinking?*
   a. orientation, preparation, incubation, illumination, verification
   b. orientation, incubation, preparation, illumination, verification
   c. preparation, orientation, incubation, verification, illumination
   d. preparation, incubation, illumination, verification, orientation

29. *Which of the following is a characteristic of the creative personality?*
   a. IQ greater than 120
   b. introversion
   c. having a narrow range of interests
   d. valuing independence

30. *Which thinking error involves ignoring the base rate?*
   a. representativeness heuristic
   b. underlying odds
   c. framing
   d. intuition

31. *When the wording of a question affects the decision a person makes, this is referred to as*
   a. representativeness.
   b. framing.
   c. base rate.
   d. emotional interferences.

32. *The operational definition of intelligence is determined by*
   a. the global capacity to act purposefully.
   b. general mental abilities.
   c. the procedures used to measure it.
   d. a person's daily behaviors.

33. *_____ refers to the mental processing of information.*
   a. Cognition
   b. Thinking
   c. Imagination
   d. Intuition

34. *Josh's coach tells the team that he knows how to win the basketball game— "Score more points than the other team!" This would be an example of a _____ solution.*
   a. specific
   b. mechanical
   c. general
   d. functional

35. *WAIS-III is to _____ as WISC-IV is to _____.*
   a. men; women
   b. intelligence; intuition
   c. performance; behavior
   d. adult; children

MOTIVATION AND EMOTION

Our behavior is energized and directed by motives and emotions. Emotions are linked to many basic adaptive behaviors, which help us survive and adjust to changing conditions.

Francis-Xavier Marit/Getty Images

Motivation

The concept of motivation refers to the ways in which our actions are initiated, sustained, directed, and terminated. Behavior can be activated by needs (push) or goals (pull).

Emotion

Emotion is a state characterized by physiological arousal, subjective feelings, and changes in outward expression (facial expressions, gestures, posture). The autonomic nervous system plays a key role in the experience of emotion. Some emotions can be disruptive, but overall they provide adaptive and survival functions.

Primary Motives

Primary motives are based on biological requirements for physical survival. Most primary motives operate to maintain **homeostasis**. They include hunger, thirst, pain avoidance, and needs for bodily function. While most of these motives occur in regular cycles, pain avoidance is **episodic**.

Maslow's Hierarchy of Needs

Maslow's hierarchy categorizes needs as basic and growth-oriented, with lower needs dominating higher ones. **Self-actualization** is expressed in **meta-needs**, closely related to intrinsic motivation. Sometimes, **extrinsic** rewards can undermine **intrinsic** motivation.

Primary Emotions

Plutchik's research indicates eight primary emotions, each of which may vary in intensity. They may also combine to produce more complex emotional experiences. **Moods** are low intensity emotional states that can last for extended periods.

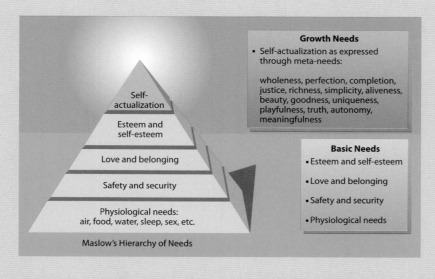

Growth Needs
- Self-actualization as expressed through meta-needs:

  wholeness, perfection, completion, justice, richness, simplicity, aliveness, beauty, goodness, uniqueness, playfulness, truth, autonomy, meaningfulness

Basic Needs
- Esteem and self-esteem
- Love and belonging
- Safety and security
- Physiological needs

Self-actualization

Esteem and self-esteem

Love and belonging

Safety and security

Physiological needs: air, food, water, sleep, sex, etc.

Maslow's Hierarchy of Needs

CHAPTER 10

Motivation and Emotion

Stimulus Motives

Stimulus drives contribute to survival by keeping us connected with the world around us. Stimulus motives appear to be innate, but they are not strictly necessary for survival. They include curiosity, activity, exploration, manipulation, and physical contact. Much behavior is related to needs for stimulation and efforts to maintain optimal levels of arousal.

Learned Motives

Learned motives, based on learned needs, goals, and drives, explain much of the diversity in human behavior. Many are related to needs for power, affiliation, approval, security, and achievement. **Social motives** are acquired through socialization and cultural conditioning. Self-confidence greatly affects motivation.

The Special Case of Hunger and Eating

Hunger is a basic physiological need influenced by an interplay of various biological factors. Overeating and undereating are often related to emotional or cultural factors.

Courtesy of Neal E. Miller, Rockefeller University.

Obesity

Obesity is the result of the interplay of internal and external influences, diet, emotions, genetics, and exercise. The best way to lose weight is **behavioral dieting**.

Eating Disorders

Anorexia nervosa and **bulimia nervosa** are serious disorders that can cause physical damage or death. They both tend to involve conflicts about self-image, self-control, and anxiety.

Emotional Intelligence

Emotional intelligence is the ability to consciously make your emotions work for you in a wide variety of life circumstances. Positive emotions tend to broaden our focus, and they encourage personal growth and social connection.

"Lie Detectors"

Polygraphs detect autonomic nervous system arousal. They cannot distinguish between lying and anxiety. Accuracy can be low.

Camay Sungu/AP/Wide World Photo

Chapter Concepts

- *Motives and goals greatly influence what we do and how we use our energies.*
- *Basic motives, such as hunger and thirst, are controlled by internal signals monitored within the brain.*
- *The most effective "diet" is one that changes eating habits and activity levels.*
- *Motivated behavior is also influenced by learned habits, external cues, and cultural values.*
- *Numerous activities are related to our needs for stimulation and our efforts to maintain comfortable levels of arousal.*
- *Many needs and motives are learned.*
- *Emotions can be disruptive, but overall they help us adapt to environmental challenges.*
- *People who are "smart" emotionally are self-aware and empathetic. They understand emotions; can manage their feelings; and use emotions to enhance thinking, decision-making, and relationships.*

Concept Review

1. The ways in which our actions are initiated, sustained, and directed is called
   a. need.
   b. drive.
   c. need-reduction.
   d. motivation.

2. Which of the following refers to an energized motivational state?
   a. need
   b. drive
   c. need-reduction
   d. motivation

3. Which of the following is the correct order for the model of motivation?
   a. need, drive, response, goal
   b. goal, need, drive, response
   c. need, response, drive, goal
   d. drive, need, response, goal

4. Your mother's homemade chocolate cake is so good, you eat a piece of it even though you aren't really hungry. This is because the _____ of the pie motivates your eating behavior in the absence of the internal need.
   a. motivational value
   b. stimulus value
   c. incentive value
   d. secondary value

5. Motives such as activity, curiosity, exploration, manipulation, and physical contact are called
   a. primary motives.
   b. stimulus motives.
   c. secondary motives.
   d. response motives.

6. Which type of motive is based on learned needs, drives, and goals?
   a. primary motive
   b. stimulus motive
   c. learned motive
   d. tertiary motive

7. The term describing the steady state in which the body has achieved optimal levels with such things as body temperature is called
   a. need.
   b. homeostasis.
   c. goal.
   d. disequilibrium.

8. Which part or function of the body is NOT involved in hunger?
   a. blood sugar levels
   b. the liver
   c. the hypothalamus
   d. the hippocampus

9. If the ventromedial hypothalamus is destroyed, the result is
   a. dramatic overeating.
   b. starvation due to not eating.
   c. hyperactivity.
   d. death.

10. According to the textbook, all of the following factors may lead to overeating EXCEPT
    a. sweetness of food.
    b. high fat content in food.
    c. high protein in food.
    d. variety of food available.

11. Behavioral dieting suggests that people do which of the following?
    a. Exercise for at least 2 hours a day.
    b. Keep track of eating habits using a "diet diary."
    c. Have snacks throughout the day to help minimize hunger.
    d. Study, talk on the phone, and participate in other activities while eating.

12. Which of the following is typical of the bulimia nervosa victim but NOT of the anorexia nervosa victim?
    a. purging
    b. normal or near-normal body weight
    c. self-evaluation unduly influenced by body weight
    d. fear of becoming fat

13. Vomiting and diarrhea are two causes of
    a. extracellular thirst.
    b. intracellular thirst.
    c. anorexia.
    d. bulimia.

14. Which of the following is an episodic drive?
    a. hunger
    b. thirst
    c. pain
    d. sleepiness

15. Which one is NOT a stimulus drive?
    a. exploration
    b. manipulation
    c. hunger
    d. curiosity

16. Low sensation seekers are
    a. selfish.
    b. more likely to smoke.
    c. independent.
    d. orderly.

17. The Yerkes-Dodson law refers to the idea that complex tasks are better accomplished at
    a. a lower level of arousal.
    b. a higher level of arousal.
    c. a moderate level of arousal.
    d. a flow state of arousal.

18. Bettie is worried about her psychology test. She imagines herself going blank, then calmly tells herself that she will handle that by focusing on one question at a time. She is practicing
    a. preparation.
    b. relaxation.
    c. rehearsal.
    d. restructuring thoughts.

19. *Which of the following is TRUE concerning circadian rhythms?*
    a. They play no role in affecting functions such as body temperature, blood pressure, and kidney function.
    b. People with shorter circadian rhythms are night people.
    c. Disruptions of the circadian clock can be overcome in just a couple of hours.
    d. Melatonin is a hormone that affects circadian rhythms.

20. *According to the _____, if a stimulus causes a strong emotion (such as fear), then an opposite emotion tends to occur when the stimulus ends (such as relief).*
    a. Yerkes-Dodson theory
    b. opponent-process theory
    c. triarchic theory
    d. Cannon-Bard theory

21. *The need for _____ is a desire to have impact on or control others.*
    a. achievement
    b. power
    c. success
    d. affiliation

22. *Maslow describes the first four levels of his hierarchy as _____ needs.*
    a. basic
    b. growth
    c. self-actualization
    d. meta

23. *Which is NOT a meta-need, according to Maslow?*
    a. wholeness
    b. justice
    c. beauty
    d. self-esteem

24. *Caleb plays the drums for his own enjoyment. What term best describes this behavior?*
    a. extrinsic motivation
    b. intrinsic motivation
    c. meta-need
    d. need for achievement

25. *Jackie's hands are shaking and her posture is tense as she prepares to give a speech. These are signs of the element of emotion called*
    a. emotional expressions.
    b. emotional feelings.
    c. physiological changes.
    d. psychokinetic activity.

26. *According to Plutchik, there are eight primary emotions. These include all but which of the following?*
    a. fear
    b. surprise
    c. love
    d. anger

27. *Some people become dizzy and faint at the sight of blood because of the*
    a. amygdala.
    b. parasympathetic system.
    c. left hemisphere.
    d. hypothalamus.

28. *Which of the following is also referred to as "fight or flight"?*
    a. sympathetic system
    b. parasympathetic system
    c. amygdala
    d. hypothalamus

29. *Which facial expression is recognized around the world?*
    a. fear
    b. anger
    c. happiness
    d. all of the above

30. *Facial expressions can be narrowed down to just three basic dimensions of activation, pleasantness-unpleasantness, and*
    a. love-hate.
    b. warm-rejecting.
    c. attention-rejection.
    d. calm-nervous.

31. *Gestures used to show what people are saying are called _____; they tend to _____ when a person is telling a lie.*
    a. emblems; increase
    b. emblems; decrease
    c. illustrators; increase
    d. illustrators; decrease

32. *According to which theory do feelings and arousal occur at the same time?*
    a. James-Lange
    b. Cannon-Bard
    c. Schachter's cognitive theory
    d. facial-feedback

33. *A person may feel anxious when approaching a particular social situation, but she attributes her anxiety to the three cups of coffee that she had just an hour earlier rather than to the social situation. Which theory of emotion does this illustrate?*
    a. James-Lange
    b. Cannon-Bard
    c. Schachter's cognitive theory
    d. facial-feedback

34. *According to your text, emotional intelligence includes*
    a. understanding emotions.
    b. perceiving emotions.
    c. managing emotions.
    d. all of the above

35. *A typical polygraph will record changes in all of the following except*
    a. breathing.
    b. heart rate.
    c. galvanic skin response.
    d. pupil dilation.

GENDER AND SEXUALITY

Sex and gender have a tremendous impact on relationships, personal identity, and health. The classification "male" or "female" is not always a simple matter, and women and men are more alike than different.

© Charlie Westerman/Getty Images

Sex

Sex refers to whether a person is biologically female or male. This determination takes into account one's **genetic sex** (XX or XY), **hormonal sex** (androgens or estrogens), **gonadal sex** (testes or ovaries), and **genital sex** (primary sex characteristics).

Gender

Gender refers to all the psychological and social characteristics associated with being male or female. **Gender identity**, one's subjective sense of being female or male, is usually stable by age 3 or 4. Gender identity is influenced by biology, socialization, and learning.

Sexual Orientation

The degree to which one is attracted emotionally and erotically to members of the same sex, opposite sex, or both sexes determines one's sexual orientation. All three orientations are part of the normal range of sexual behavior, and homosexual women and men do not differ psychologically from heterosexuals.

Sexual Behaviors

Sexuality is a natural part of being human, and a wide variety of sexual behaviors are possible. "Normal" sexual behavior is defined differently by various cultures. **Masturbation** is a regular feature of the sex lives of many people.

Male-Female Differences

Men and women are more alike than different on most psychological dimensions. Most observed male-female differences result from **gender role socialization**, in which parents encourage boys in instrumental behaviors and girls in expressive behaviors. **Gender role stereotypes** continue to have impact on women and men, including playing a role in **rape**.

Androgyny

About one third of all people possess both masculine and feminine traits (androgynous), and about half are traditionally feminine or masculine. Psychological androgyny is related to greater behavioral adaptability and flexibility.

Sexual Response

Sexual response can be divided into four phases—**excitement**, **plateau**, **orgasm**, and **resolution**. While sexual arousal is related to the body's **erogenous zones**, mental and emotional reactions are the source of sexual responsiveness.

Sexual Disorders

The most common **paraphilias** are **pedophilia** and **exhibitionism**. Since most paraphilias involve compulsive behavior, they tend to emotionally handicap people. Compulsive or coercive behaviors are psychologically unhealthy.

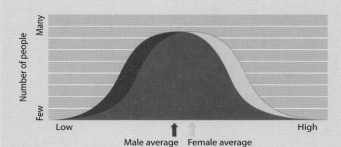

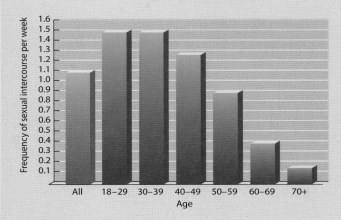

Gender and Sexuality

Safer Sex

Most adults favor greater freedom of choice for themselves, including choice about sexual freedom. The increase in sexually transmitted diseases (STDs) and HIV/AIDS creates new and compelling reasons for caution in sexual behavior.

Sexual Problems

Sexual dysfunctions are far more common than many people realize. Disorders can affect different aspects of sexual function—desire, arousal, orgasm—or may be related to sexual pain. Most sexual adjustment problems are closely related to the general health of a couple's relationship. Good communication is essential. Behavioral methods and counseling have been developed to alleviate many sexual problems.

Chapter Concepts

- *Male and female are not simple either/or categories. Sexual identity is complex, multifaceted, and influenced by biology, socialization, and learning.*
- *Women and men are more alike than they are different. The core of humanity in each person is more important than superficial gender differences.*
- *Androgynous individuals have both masculine and feminine gender traits, all combinations that tend to be adaptive and desirable.*
- *All sexual orientations have similar underlying factors (heredity, biology, and socialization).*
- *An understanding of human sexual response contributes to responsible and satisfying sexual behavior.*
- *Adults normally engage in a wide variety of sexual behaviors. However, coercive or compulsive sexual behaviors are emotionally unhealthy.*
- *Each person must take responsibility for practicing safer sex and for choosing when, where, and with whom to express his or her sexuality.*
- *Solutions exist for many sexual adjustment problems, but good communication and a healthy relationship are the real keys to sexual satisfaction.*
- *Most touching is nonsexual. However, touching tends to be highly restricted in North America because of social norms and fears that touching will be perceived as erotic or inappropriate.*

Concept Review

1. The psychological and social aspects of being male or female are known as
   a. sex.
   b. gender.
   c. androgyny.
   d. sexuality.

2. Which of the following is NOT a primary sex characteristic?
   a. ovaries
   b. testes
   c. breasts
   d. vagina

3. When a woman reaches _____, she can, soon after, bear children.
   a. menarche
   b. menopause
   c. age 30
   d. age 40

4. Which term refers to the end of regular monthly fertility cycles?
   a. menarche
   b. menopause
   c. age 30
   d. age 40

5. The predominance of androgens or estrogens is called
   a. genetic sex.
   b. gonadal sex.
   c. hormonal sex.
   d. genital sex.

6. Estrogen is to _____ as androgen is to _____.
   a. sex; gender
   b. biology; culture
   c. testes; gonads
   d. female; male

7. Which term refers to a problem leading to a female child born with genitals that are more male than female?
   a. androgen insensitivity
   b. hermaphroditism
   c. androgenital syndrome
   d. biological biasing effect

8. The favored pattern of behavior expected of each sex is
   a. gender role.
   b. gender identity.
   c. gender typing.
   d. gender stereotype.

9. Which term refers to the oversimplified beliefs one can have concerning what men and women are really like?
   a. gender role
   b. gender identity
   c. gender typing
   d. gender role stereotype

10. Sons are encouraged to engage in _____ behavior, whereas daughters are encouraged to engage in _____ behavior.
    a. instrumental; expressive
    b. expressive; instrumental
    c. inappropriate; appropriate
    d. appropriate; inappropriate

11. Androgyny refers to having
    a. ambiguous sexual organs.
    b. masculine personality traits.
    c. feminine personality traits.
    d. both feminine and masculine personality traits.

12. Human erogenous zones can include the
    a. genitals.
    b. mouth.
    c. entire skin surface.
    d. all of the above

13. Our sexual behavior is guided by unspoken mental plans called
    a. sexual plans.
    b. sexual scripts.
    c. sexual roles.
    d. gender roles.

14. A woman's subjective feelings of sexual arousal seemed to be closely tied with her
    a. emotional response to erotic cues.
    b. physical response to erotic cues.
    c. sexual experience.
    d. sexual fantasies.

15. Alcohol, in large dosages,
    a. is an aphrodisiac.
    b. strengthens inhibitions.
    c. decreases sexual desire.
    d. acts as a stimulant.

16. Which of the following statements about masturbation is FALSE?
    a. Infants do it.
    b. Men do it more often than women.
    c. It may cause blindness if done too often.
    d. It continues throughout the lifespan.

17. Sexual orientation has been shown to be determined by
    a. heredity.
    b. biology.
    c. social, cultural, and psychological influences.
    d. all of the above

18. Which of the following is NOT a myth about homosexuality or homosexual persons?
    a. They try to convert others.
    b. They may be subjected to homophobia.
    c. They are mentally ill.
    d. Their children often become gay.

19. In the _____ phase, physical arousal intensifies.
    a. excitement
    b. plateau
    c. orgasm
    d. resolution

20. Which two stages might be regularly repeated by approximately 15 percent of women during the same sexual encounter?
    a. plateau and orgasm
    b. excitement and plateau
    c. orgasm and resolution
    d. excitement and resolution

21. *A man cannot have another orgasm until the _____ has passed.*
    a. plateau phase
    b. refractory period
    c. excitement phase
    d. orgasmic experience

22. *The mark of true sexual deviation from a psychological perspective is*
    a. statistical abnormality.
    b. a nonstandard variation.
    c. compulsiveness and destructiveness.
    d. atypicality.

23. *The "peeping Tom" paraphilia is called*
    a. pedophilia.
    b. frotteurism.
    c. transvestism.
    d. voyeurism.

24. *Which term refers to sexually touching a nonconsenting person in a public place?*
    a. pedophilia
    b. frotteurism
    c. transvestism
    d. voyeurism

25. *Which paraphilia is associated with the highest repeat rate among sex offenders?*
    a. pedophilia
    b. voyeurism
    c. exhibitionism
    d. sado-masochism

26. *Which statement about pedophiles is FALSE?*
    a. Most act alone.
    b. Most assaults happen outside the home.
    c. Many gain access as child caretakers.
    d. Bribes and gifts are used as lures.

27. *Which of the following is NOT a rape myth?*
    a. When a woman says no, she means no.
    b. A woman who is dressed attractively, is alone, and is in public is "asking for it."
    c. Many women actually enjoy being raped.
    d. A woman who goes home with a man on a first date is interested in sex.

28. *If you have a sexually transmitted disease but are not experiencing symptoms,*
    a. you will still know that you have it.
    b. you cannot pass it to a partner.
    c. you do not need treatment.
    d. you can still give it to another person.

29. *Which of the following groups are populations at risk for HIV infection?*
    a. homosexual and bisexual men
    b. heterosexuals
    c. hemophiliacs
    d. All of these groups are at greater risk for HIV.

30. *Which of the following is NOT considered a risky sexual behavior?*
    a. anal sex
    b. unprotected sex
    c. having two or more sexual partners
    d. open-mouth kissing

31. *Dyspareunia and vaginismus are*
    a. desire disorders.
    b. sexual pain disorders.
    c. orgasm disorders.
    d. arousal disorders.

32. *Which of the following disorder types are often treated with a technique called sensate focus?*
    a. desire disorders
    b. sexual pain disorders
    c. orgasmic disorders
    d. arousal disorders

33. *Females with sexual arousal disorder*
    a. show excessive physical arousal to sexual stimulation.
    b. show little or no response to sexual stimulation.
    c. are unresponsive to the context of their relationships.
    d. experience muscle spasms in the vagina that prevent orgasm.

34. *Which of the following elements does sex therapist Barry McCarthy indicate as being necessary for a healthy sexual relationship?*
    a. sexual anticipation
    b. valuing one's sexuality
    c. valuing intimacy
    d. all of the above

35. *Male infidelity being historically seen as more acceptable than female infidelity is an example of*
    a. a double standard.
    b. "sowing oats."
    c. sexual freedom.
    d. a sexual revolution.

PERSONALITY

Personality refers to a consistent yet unique pattern of thinking, emotions, and behavior. Measures of personality reveal individual differences and help predict future behavior of individuals.

David Young-Wolff/PhotoEdit

Understanding Personality

Developing an understanding of personality involves identifying traits, evaluating mental processes, taking note of the effects of learning and the social situation, and knowing how people perceive themselves.

Character, Temperament, and Traits

Character is not the same thing as personality. The term *character* implies a value judgment about desirability or undesirability of behaviors. Temperament reflects the hereditary aspects of one's personality. Traits are lasting personal qualities that are inferred from one's behavior. Heredity contributes significantly to personality traits.

Changing Personality

Because learned experiences and thought patterns are key ingredients of personality, techniques have been developed to assist in changing personality. **Shyness**, for example, can be reduced by replacing self-defeating beliefs and by learning social skills.

Personality Theories

Four major perspectives attempt to explain personality.

Trait Theories

These theories identify lasting and consistent personal characteristics and attempt to determine how they relate to behavior. Cattell suggests there are 16 underlying source traits. The **five-factor model** of personality identifies five universal dimensions of personality.

		Low Scorers	High Scorers
1	Extroversion	Loner Quiet Passive Reserved	Joiner Talkative Active Affectionate
2	Agreeableness	Suspicious Critical Ruthless Irritable	Trusting Lenient Soft-hearted Good-natured
3	Conscientiousness	Negligent Lazy Disorganized Late	Conscientious Hard-working Well-organized Punctual
4	Neuroticism	Calm Even-tempered Comfortable Unemotional	Worried Temperamental Self-conscious Emotional
5	Openness to experience	Down-to-earth Uncreative Conventional Uncurious	Imaginative Creative Original Curious

Personality Testing

Interviews, direct observation, questionnaires, and projective tests are used to evaluate personality. Each method of assessment has advantages and disadvantages; therefore, they are often used in combination.

Behavioral Theories

These theories focus on the effects of learning, conditioning, and situational influences in the development of personality. **Social learning theory** expands this perspective to include thinking, expectations, and other mental processes.

Personality Types

Personality types group people into categories on the basis of shared traits. Although they may oversimplify personality, types can be useful as a shorthand way to describe people (as in Type A and Type B personalities).

Self-Concept and Self-Esteem

People's self-concept consists of all their ideas, perceptions, and feelings about who they are. Self-esteem is a person's self-evaluation of her or his worth. Self-concepts have a significant impact on behavior, and self-esteem is strongly influenced by culture.

Psychodynamic Theories

These theories emphasize internal forces and mental activities that shape personality. Personality consists of the **id**, **ego**, and **superego**, which operate at **conscious**, **preconscious**, and **unconscious** levels. Personality development progresses through five stages.

Humanistic Theories

These theories stress subjective experience, free choice, and **self-actualization**. **Self-image** and evaluation are key components in personality development, and the approach emphasizes positive aspects of human nature.

CHAPTER 12

Personality

Andre Forget/AP/Wide World Photo

Chapter Concepts

- *Each of us displays consistent behavior patterns that define our own personalities and allow us to predict how other people will act.*
- *Personality can be understood by identifying traits, by probing mental conflicts and dynamics, by noting the effects of prior learning and social situations, and by knowing how people perceive themselves.*
- *The terms temperament, character, and personality each have different meanings.*
- *Psychologists use interviews, direct observation, questionnaires, and projective tests to measure and assess personality.*
- *Different psychological theorists have developed a variety of approaches to looking at personality.*
- *Shyness is related to public self-consciousness and other psychological factors that can be altered, thereby helping some people overcome their shyness.*

Concept Review

1. *Foundation is to _____ as house is to _____.*
   a. personality; character
   b. character; temperament
   c. temperament; personality
   d. none of the above

2. *The disadvantage to personality types is that*
   a. they don't really exist.
   b. they tend to oversimplify personality.
   c. they are fairly unstable.
   d. there are far too many.

3. *Which of the following is true concerning self-concept?*
   a. It is quickly revised as a result of new experiences.
   b. It guides what we pay attention to, remember, and think about.
   c. It does not affect our behavior and personal adjustment.
   d. Self-esteem refers to the quantity of one's self-concept.

4. *_____ self-esteem is based on an accurate appraisal of your strengths and weaknesses.*
   a. Insightful
   b. Negative
   c. Positive
   d. Genuine

5. *The traits that are shared by most members of a cultural group are called _____ traits.*
   a. common
   b. individual
   c. central
   d. cardinal

6. *Abraham Lincoln is often referred to as "Honest Abe" due to the trait of honesty being evident in everything he did. Honesty would likely be considered a _____ trait for Abraham Lincoln.*
   a. common
   b. individual
   c. central
   d. cardinal

7. *Sandy is a very friendly person who likes Chinese food. Sandy's friendliness is most likely a _____ trait, whereas her preference for Chinese cuisine is most likely a(n) _____ trait.*
   a. common; individual
   b. cardinal; central
   c. central; secondary
   d. surface; source

8. *If, through your studies, you find that people who are extroverted are typically sociable, talkative, and outgoing, you may have performed what Cattell referred to as a*
   a. surface interview.
   b. factor analysis.
   c. common assessment.
   d. secondary pf.

9. *The 16 PF is designed to measure*
   a. central traits.
   b. source traits.
   c. surface traits.
   d. cardinal traits.

10. *Joan is very emotional and worries constantly. She would probably score high on the measure of which of the Big Five trait dimensions?*
    a. agreeableness
    b. conscientiousness
    c. neuroticism
    d. openness to experience

11. *Which of the following dimensions refers to a person's willingness to try new ideas and new ways of doing things?*
    a. agreeableness
    b. conscientiousness
    c. neuroticism
    d. openness to experience

12. *A student who studies continuously throughout the semester, turns in all work on time, and shows up to every class may be considered high on what Big Five personality dimension?*
    a. agreeableness
    b. conscientiousness
    c. neuroticism
    d. openness to experience

13. *Joe is fairly calm in the classroom, but when his teacher sees him at a basketball game, he is cheering and boisterous. This seeming change in personality is probably due to*
    a. the trait-situation interaction.
    b. Joe's lack of consistency.
    c. beer.
    d. peer pressure.

14. *If a test measures what it purports to measure, it has*
    a. reliability.
    b. validity.
    c. objectivity.
    d. significance.

15. *According to Freud, the _____ is an innate biological instinct and operates on the pleasure principle.*
    a. id
    b. ego
    c. superego
    d. conscience

16. *Which term did Freud consider to be the "executive" of personality?*
    a. id
    b. ego
    c. superego
    d. conscience

17. *Which part of the personality might be referred to as your "internalized parent"?*
    a. id
    b. ego
    c. superego
    d. conscience

18. *This is the level of awareness in which material can be easily brought to awareness.*
    a. conscious
    b. unconscious
    c. preconscious
    d. id

19. Which of the following is NOT one of Freud's psychosexual stages?
    a. oral
    b. anal
    c. phallic
    d. erogenous

20. In which stage would Freud likely find a person fixated if they regularly bit other people or items?
    a. oral
    b. anal
    c. phallic
    d. latency

21. Which of Freud's followers rejected Freud's claim that "anatomy is destiny"?
    a. Adler
    b. Horney
    c. Jung
    d. Erikson

22. Which theorist believed that the ego "wore a mask, or persona"?
    a. Adler
    b. Horney
    c. Jung
    d. Erikson

23. Which of the following is not an archetype?
    a. animus
    b. anima
    c. self
    d. superego

24. According to Dollard and Miller, _____ make up the structure of personality.
    a. drives
    b. habits
    c. cues
    d. rewards

25. Which of the four critical situations, according to Dollard and Miller, may create a basic passive or active orientation to the world?
    a. early feeding experiences
    b. toilet training
    c. sex training
    d. learning to express anger

26. Learning theorists believe that sex training is accomplished primarily by the child's
    a. resolution of the Oedipal conflict.
    b. need for positive regard.
    c. identification and imitation of models.
    d. natural cognitive awareness of roles.

27. Which is NOT a focus of humanism?
    a. free choice
    b. unconscious urges
    c. subjective experience
    d. self-actualization

28. According to Maslow, a self-actualizer would be or possess which of the following?
    a. entirely self-oriented
    b. dependent
    c. uncomfortable being alone
    d. nonhostile sense of humor

29. Rogers' concept of the _____ is most similar to Freud's concept of the ego ideal.
    a. real self
    b. ideal self
    c. congruent person
    d. incongruent person

30. According to Rogers, people who receive _____ are most likely to develop _____.
    a. conditional positive regard; organismic valuing
    b. unconditional positive regard; organismic valuing
    c. unconditional positive regard; conditions of worth
    d. conditions of worth; positive regard

31. The MMPI-2 is an example of a
    a. structured interview.
    b. behavioral assessment.
    c. personality questionnaire.
    d. projective test.

32. The MMPI-2 contains _____ scales to detect attempts by the test taker to be dishonest or answer randomly.
    a. reliability
    b. nonclinical
    c. psychasthenia
    d. validity

33. Having police officer candidates shoot at targets at a firing range is an example of what type of personality assessment?
    a. structured interview
    b. situational testing
    c. projective testing
    d. unstructured interview

34. Which of the following is/are criticism(s) of projective personality tests?
    a. lack of objectivity
    b. low reliability
    c. low validity
    d. all of the above

35. According to a study of inmates at a California prison, sudden murderers are very likely to be
    a. masculine and aggressive.
    b. impulsive.
    c. passive, shy, and restrained.
    d. Type A.

HEALTH, STRESS, AND COPING

Health is affected greatly by lifestyle and behavior patterns, especially those related to stress. **Health psychology** studies how personal habits and behavior patterns can lead to illness and death or promote health and **wellness**.

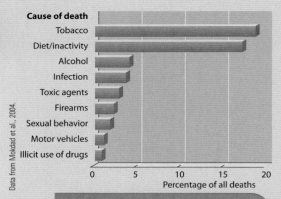

Cause of death

Tobacco	
Diet/inactivity	
Alcohol	
Infection	
Toxic agents	
Firearms	
Sexual behavior	
Motor vehicles	
Illicit use of drugs	

Percentage of all deaths

Data from Mokdad et al., 2004.

Stress

Stress is the mental and physical condition that occurs when a person must adapt to environmental demands. Stress is not always "bad," but it can be a major risk factor when prolonged or severe. Stress is often a matter of how a person perceives and reacts to events.

Stress Reaction

A stress reaction begins with autonomic system arousal. The **general adaptation syndrome** explains bodily reactions in response to prolonged stress.

Stress Reduction

A variety of cognitive and behavioral stress management techniques can be used to manage stress and reduce its effects, including exercise, meditation, progressive relaxation, guided imagery, biofeedback, journaling, getting organized, and learning to use coping statements to combat upsetting thoughts.

Reuters/Corbis

People and Environment Interactions

People must always interact with the environments in which they live, and stress can result from these interactions. Events involving pressure, lack of control, unpredictability, and intense or repeated emotional shock tend to be the most stressful. Stress is intensified when a person interprets a situation as a threat or does not feel competent to cope with the situation.

Behavioral Risk Factors

A small number of behavioral patterns account for the majority of common health problems. Personal health habits formed early in life greatly affect health, happiness, and life expectancy throughout adulthood. Health psychologists try to help people remove behavioral risk factors and increase health-promoting behaviors.

Tim Pannell/Corbis

CHAPTER 13

Health, Stress, and Coping

Stress and Health

The body's reaction to stress can directly damage internal organs. Stress lowers the body's resistance to disease by weakening the immune system. Intense stress may cause psychosomatic problems. Intense daily hassles can affect psychological health.

Personality and Stress

Personality characteristics influence the amount of stress a person experiences and the risk of illness. **Type A** personalities are more prone to heart attacks, while **hardy** personality types appear more resistant to stress effects. Optimism and social support help buffer stress.

Good Stress

Stress is not necessarily "bad." Some forms of stress are related to positive activities, such as engaging in recreational activities, dating, or moving to a sought-after job. This form of "good" stress is called **eustress**.

Purestock/SuperStock

Greg Epperson/Photolibrary

Stressors, Appraisal, and Coping

A stressor is the condition or event in the environment that challenges or threatens a person. When faced with the stressor, a person appraises the threat via **primary** and **secondary appraisal**. To cope, a person might choose **problem-focused coping** or **emotion-focused coping**, including **defense mechanisms**.

Frustration

Frustration is a negative emotional state that occurs when people are prevented from reaching desired goals. Behavioral reactions may be positive (e.g., persistence) or negative (e.g., aggression, displace aggression, withdrawal).

Conflict

Responses that are followed by punishment become less frequent. Punishment tends to produce **escape learning** and **avoidance learning**.

Pressure

Pressure happens when a person must meet urgent external demands or expectations. Pressure is particularly common in work settings. Chronic job stress sometimes results in **burnout**.

Chapter Concepts

- *A variety of personal habits and behavior patterns affect health.*
- *Maintaining good health is a personal responsibility, not a matter of luck. Wellness is based on minimizing risk factors and engaging in health-promoting behaviors.*
- *Stress is a normal part of life; however, it is also a major risk factor for illness and disease.*
- *Although some events are more stressful than others, stress always represents an interaction between people and the environments in which they live.*
- *Personality characteristics affect the amount of stress a person experiences and the subsequent risk of illness.*
- *The body's reactions to stress can directly damage internal organs, and stress impairs the body's immune system, increasing susceptibility to disease.*
- *The damaging effects of stress can be reduced with stress-management techniques.*

Concept Review

1. Using behavioral principles to promote health and prevent illness is called
   a. health psychology.
   b. behavioral medicine.
   c. lifestyle management.
   d. health promotion.

2. Which is NOT a behavioral risk factor?
   a. high levels of stress
   b. overeating
   c. getting 7 to 8 hours of sleep each night
   d. excess sun exposure

3. In the Kolbe, Collins, and Cortese (1997) study, what percentage of high school students had five or more drinks the previous month?
   a. 30
   b. 50
   c. 65
   d. 10

4. The disease-prone personality is
   a. chronically depressed.
   b. anxious.
   c. hostile.
   d. all of the above

5. Each of the following is a health-promoting behavior mentioned in your textbook EXCEPT
   a. exercising 30 minutes per day.
   b. reducing alcohol intake to 2 to 3 drinks per day.
   c. maintaining a diet high in fruit, vegetables, and fish.
   d. managing stress.

6. Which of the following, according to the textbook, is an emotional sign of stress?
   a. depression
   b. anxiety
   c. poor judgment
   d. frequent illness

7. Part of the reason a professor's job is so stressful is that he or she never knows whether students will be cooperative or uncooperative in the classroom. This is an example of
   a. unpredictability.
   b. uncontrollableness.
   c. pressure.
   d. intensity.

8. A _____ is a condition or event that challenges or threatens a person.
   a. stipulation
   b. health hazard
   c. pressure
   d. stressor

9. Marie, a nurse, no longer cares about her patients and treats them as objects—annoying objects, at that. She is suffering from which aspect of burnout?
   a. cynicism
   b. emotional exhaustion
   c. reduced personal accomplishment
   d. secondary onset

10. Deciding what you can do about a threatening situation is a(n)
    a. primary appraisal.
    b. secondary appraisal.
    c. tertiary appraisal.
    d. inclusive appraisal.

11. Jerry called the police when his neighbors got too noisy at their late-night party and refused to hear his pleas for them to hold it down. He is using _____ coping.
    a. problem-focused
    b. emotion-focused
    c. conflict-focused
    d. frustration-conflict oriented

12. Engaging in meditation is an example of what type of coping?
    a. problem-focused
    b. emotion-focused
    c. conflict-focused
    d. frustration-conflict oriented

13. Austin's marriage proposal was met with laughter and a resounding "no thanks." This is an example of
    a. an external frustration.
    b. a personal frustration.
    c. persistence.
    d. a nonsocial frustration.

14. Which of the following is NOT a factor listed in your textbook that may increase frustration?
    a. strength of blocked motive
    b. urgency of blocked motive
    c. intelligence of frustrated person
    d. importance of frustration

15. While not always the first reaction to frustration, _____ is/are one of the most frequent responses.
    a. persistence
    b. varied responses
    c. aggression
    d. more vigorous efforts

16. If you choose to escape frustration, you might
    a. leave the situation entirely.
    b. pretend not to care.
    c. abuse drugs.
    d. all of the above

17. Annie wants to see the new James Bond movie, but she also wants to go to the concert in the park. She only has the one night off and must decide between the two. This is an example of
    a. approach-approach conflict.
    b. approach-avoidance conflict.
    c. double approach-avoidance conflict.
    d. avoidance-avoidance conflict.

18. Which of the following would apply if you had to decide between getting a root canal or having a tooth extracted?
    a. approach-approach conflict
    b. approach-avoidance conflict
    c. double approach-avoidance conflict
    d. avoidance-avoidance conflict

19. Luke refused to believe that he had cancer, even when shown the results of the tests. It is possible that Luke is experiencing
    a. repression.
    b. reaction formation.
    c. denial.
    d. projection.

20. Which defense mechanism is relevant to a jealous husband who has a mistress on the side?
    a. repression
    b. reaction formation
    c. denial
    d. projection

21. "I couldn't turn my paper in on time because my printer broke last night." This is probably an example of
    a. rationalization.
    b. compensation.
    c. regression.
    d. sublimation.

22. Gary repeats to himself, "I am good enough, smart enough, and dog gone it, people like me," whenever he feels depressed. This might be an example of
    a. a coping statement.
    b. a positive instance.
    c. stress imagination.
    d. sublimation.

23. Both learned helplessness and depression are marked by
    a. moodiness.
    b. feelings of power.
    c. hopelessness.
    d. aggression.

24. Which is NOT a reason that students get the blues?
    a. pressure to choose a career
    b. isolation and loneliness
    c. increased freedoms and decreased supervision
    d. alcohol abuse

25. Which of the following is an immune response caused by stress?
    a. decrease in white blood cells
    b. increases in inflammation
    c. decreases in red blood cells
    d. both a and b

26. Whenever Rick is in the dentist's chair, he tries to picture himself on the beach, with the noise of the surf nearby. He is using the stress management technique of
    a. exercise.
    b. progressive relaxation.
    c. guided imagery.
    d. meditation.

27. The pattern of acculturative stress that involves a person adopting a new culture as his or her own is called
    a. integration.
    b. separation.
    c. assimilation.
    d. marginalization.

28. _____ are when psychological factors contribute to damaging changes in bodily functioning.
    a. Hypochondriacal disorders
    b. Somatoform disorders
    c. Psychosomatic disorders
    d. Psychoceramic disorders

29. Among the most common psychosomatic problems are
    a. gastrointestinal problems.
    b. heart problems.
    c. allergic reactions.
    d. circulatory problems.

30. Biofeedback has been successful in treating
    a. migraines.
    b. drug abuse.
    c. anxiety.
    d. phobias.

31. The lethal characteristic of Type A is
    a. time urgency.
    b. hostility.
    c. ambition.
    d. competitiveness.

32. The hardy personality
    a. is not very serious about work.
    b. attributes events to luck.
    c. sees problems as challenges.
    d. is Type A.

33. In which stage of the GAS would you experience an appearance of normality?
    a. alarm
    b. resistance
    c. exhaustion
    d. mobilization

34. Which of the following stages is typified by high levels of adrenal hormones?
    a. alarm
    b. resistance
    c. exhaustion
    d. mobilization

35. In which of the following stages would stress hormones be depleted?
    a. alarm
    b. resistance
    c. exhaustion
    d. mobilization

PSYCHOLOGICAL DISORDERS

Psychopathology refers to maladaptive behavior, as well as the scientific study of mental disorders. Psychological disorders need to be classified, explained, and treated. They are complex, and many have more than one cause.

What Is Abnormal?

Judgments of normality are relative, influenced by context and culture. Two elements of abnormal behavior are maladaptiveness and loss of self-control. Other factors may be considered in making a psychological diagnosis, including subjective discomfort, statistical abnormality, and social nonconformity.

Risk Factors

Risk factors for mental disorders can be social, familial, psychological, and biological.

Brent Stirton/The Image Bank/Getty Images

Psychotic and Delusional Disorders

Psychosis is a break with reality marked by a variety of severe problems. **Organic psychoses** are based on injuries or diseases of the brain; some common causes are drug abuse and dementia. Delusional disorders are based primarily on the presence of deeply held false beliefs.

Schizophrenia

Schizophrenia involves delusions, hallucinations, communication difficulties, and a split between thought and emotion. Heredity is a major factor, but environmental factors increase risk. The dominant explanation of this disorder is the **stress-vulnerability model**.

Anxiety, Dissociative, and Somatoform Disorders

Anxiety disorders include phobias, panic disorder, generalized anxiety, and posttraumatic stress disorder. Dissociative disorders may take the form of amnesia, fugue, or multiple identities, and somatoform disorders involve physical complaints that mimic diseases or disability.

Mood Disorders

Mood disorders involve disturbances of mood or emotion, producing manic or depressive states that may include psychotic features. Major disorders are partially explained by genetic vulnerability and brain chemistry, but other important factors are emotional and cognitive.

Depressive Disorders

There are many types of depression. **Dysthymic disorder** is long lasting, but moderate. **Cyclothymic disorder** involves moderate swings between depression and elation. **Seasonal affective disorder** occurs during winter months.

Personality Disorders

People with personality disorders have persistent, maladaptive personality patterns. **Sociopathy** is a type of personality disorder in which the person lacks a conscience and is emotionally cold and manipulative.

Suicide

Suicide is a common cause of death that can often be prevented. Suicide is statistically related to factors such as age, gender, and marital status. To help prevent suicide, know the common characteristics of suicidal thoughts and feelings and be prepared to establish rapport and offer support, acceptance, and caring.

Curt Borgwardt/Corbis Sygma

Classifying Mental Disorders

Psychological problems are classified using the *Diagnostic and Statistical Manual of Mental Disorders (DSM)*. The *DSM* standardizes terminology, organizes disorders into categories, provides statistical data, and establishes diagnostic criteria.

Insanity

Insanity is a legal term referring to a mental inability to manage one's own affairs or to be aware of the consequences of one's actions.

Bruce Ely

Peter Granser/Laif/Aurora Photos

Major Mood Disorders

Major depressive disorder involves extreme sadness and despondency. **Bipolar disorders** combine mania and depression.

Psychological Disorders

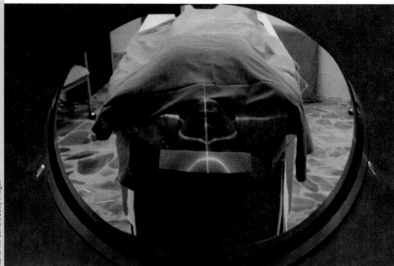

Gabriel M. Covian/Getty Images

Chapter Concepts

- *Psychological disorders damage the quality of life, in varying degrees, for many people.*
- *Psychopathology, which involves identifying, classifying, and explaining psychological disorders, is worthwhile and necessary.*
- *Psychologically unhealthy behavior is maladaptive, and it involves a loss of adequate control over thoughts, feelings, and actions.*
- *Maladaptive behavior patterns, unhealthy personality types, and excessive levels of anxiety underlie many mental disorders.*
- *The most severe forms of psychopathology involve emotional extremes or a break with reality.*
- *Psychological disorders are complex and have multiple causes.*
- *Suicide is a relatively common cause of death. In many cases it can be prevented.*

Concept Review

1. The fact that a sociopath often feels no remorse highlights the shortcomings of using _____ as a definition of abnormality.
   a. subjective discomfort
   b. statistical definitions
   c. situational context
   d. cultural relativity

2. A person with a PhD in psychology might be considered abnormal by which criterion discussed in the text?
   a. situational context
   b. statistical abnormality
   c. subjective discomfort
   d. cultural relativity

3. One of the two core features of abnormality is that it is maladaptive and
   a. statistically abnormal.
   b. a social nonconformity.
   c. involves a loss of control of one's behavior, thoughts, or emotions.
   d. culturally determined.

4. Into which of the following disorder categories would a person who has a severe loss of contact with reality fall?
   a. dissociative
   b. somatoform
   c. mood
   d. psychotic

5. Which category would include the hypochondriac?
   a. dissociative
   b. somatoform
   c. mood
   d. psychosis

6. Neurosis is an antiquated term that historically referred to symptoms involving
   a. dissociation.
   b. psychosis.
   c. anxiety.
   d. substance abuse.

7. Jeff is a homeless man, living on the streets in a crowded city. Which of the following risk factors is he facing?
   a. social conditions
   b. family factors
   c. psychological factors
   d. biological factors

8. Which core feature of psychosis involves the holding of false beliefs?
   a. confabulation
   b. perseveration
   c. hallucinations
   d. delusions

9. Which of the following types of schizophrenia is associated with unresponsiveness, posturing, and mutism?
   a. disorganized
   b. paranoid
   c. catatonic
   d. undifferentiated

10. Which disorder refers to a person who suffers from low self-confidence and allows others to run his or her life?
    a. histrionic
    b. antisocial
    c. dependent
    d. paranoid

11. Which of the following statements about the antisocial personality is FALSE?
    a. They lack a conscience.
    b. They are at times referred to as sociopaths or psychopaths.
    c. They are, at times, charming.
    d. They are, typically, crazed murderers.

12. If you are extremely worried and anxious for 6 months, you are probably suffering from
    a. generalized anxiety disorder.
    b. panic disorder.
    c. phobic disorder.
    d. obsessive-compulsive disorder.

13. Fear of enclosed spaces would be categorized as a(n) _____ phobia.
    a. animal
    b. natural environment
    c. social
    d. specific

14. Elizabeth suffers from sudden anxiety attacks that produce overwhelming feelings of dread. These attacks become so intense that she does not leave her house for fear of having them in public. What disorder would a clinician most likely diagnose her as having?
    a. generalized anxiety disorder
    b. panic disorder without agoraphobia
    c. panic disorder with agoraphobia
    d. social phobia

15. Sheila has trouble getting to work on time each morning because she repeatedly checks the doors to see that they are really locked. She is probably suffering from a(n) _____ disorder.
    a. generalized anxiety
    b. dissociative
    c. somatoform
    d. obsessive-compulsive

16. Which of the following disorders would apply to a person who has amnesia?
    a. generalized anxiety
    b. dissociative
    c. somatoform
    d. obsessive-compulsive

17. The anxiety reduction hypothesis is an explanation of anxiety disorders in which of the following perspectives?
    a. psychodynamic
    b. humanistic-existential
    c. behavioral
    d. cognitive

18. Tyron believes he is seeing bats flying around his apartment even though no one else can see them. This is an example of
    a. delusional thinking.
    b. personality disintegration.
    c. hallucinatory thinking.
    d. disturbed communication.

19. Dementia can be caused by
    a. Alzheimer's disease.
    b. poor circulation.
    c. shrinking of the brain.
    d. all of the above

20. A man believes an actress he saw on television is deeply in love with him, even though he has never met her before. The man is suffering from what type of delusional disorder?
    a. jealous type
    b. persecutory type
    c. erotomanic type
    d. grandiose type

21. Brendon goes to the doctor, complaining that his body smells funny and that he is rotting inside. He is probably suffering from a(n)
    a. grandiose type delusion.
    b. jealous type delusion.
    c. somatic type delusion.
    d. erotomanic type delusion.

22. Sandy once met a man who introduced himself as the President of the United States. Because she was touring a mental hospital at the time, and the man was a patient, we can assume that he had which of the following delusions?
    a. grandiose type delusion
    b. jealous type delusion
    c. somatic type delusion
    d. erotomanic type delusion

23. Men are more likely to _____ suicide while women are more likely to _____ suicide.
    a. threaten; fake
    b. attempt; complete
    c. complete; attempt
    d. none of the above

24. If you think there are aliens in your attic, it's a(n) _____; if you see them, it's a(n) _____.
    a. delusion; hallucination
    b. hallucination; delusion
    c. hallucination; hallucination
    d. delusion; delusion

25. Which of the following is NOT a symptom of schizophrenia?
    a. selective attention
    b. mania
    c. delusions
    d. hallucinations

26. Which of the following is not a major risk factor for suicide as identified in your text?
    a. prior suicide attempt
    b. extroverted and social behavior
    c. family history of suicide
    d. severe anxiety

27. Psychological problems are classified and diagnosed by using the
    a. MMPI-2
    b. DSM-IV-TR
    c. ICM-III
    d. APA

28. The textbook cites each of the following as an environmental cause of schizophrenia EXCEPT
    a. exposure to influenza during pregnancy.
    b. early sexual abuse.
    c. deviant familial communication patterns.
    d. low socioeconomic status.

29. Which of the following neurotransmitters is implicated as a biological cause of schizophrenia?
    a. acetylcholine
    b. serotonin
    c. dopamine
    d. GABA

30. Which of the following is the most damaging?
    a. dysthymic disorder
    b. cyclothymic disorder
    c. reactive depression
    d. major depressive disorder

31. Sharon was hospitalized when she cut her wrists in an attempted suicide. While in the hospital, she was mostly deeply depressed, with occasional bouts of hypomania. This would be _____ disorder.
    a. major depressive
    b. bipolar I
    c. bipolar II
    d. affective psychosis

32. If Laurie developed a moderately severe depression within two months of giving birth to her daughter, she might be diagnosed with
    a. maternity blues.
    b. postpartum depression.
    c. bipolar II.
    d. depression accompanied by psychosis.

33. Which of the following neurotransmitters/hormones has been implicated in seasonal depressions?
    a. serotonin
    b. GABA
    c. melatonin
    d. acetylcholine

34. _____ is the scientific study of mental, emotional, and behavioral disorders.
    a. Psychosymptomology
    b. Psychopathology
    c. Mental disorder
    d. Abnormal psychology

35. Insanity is determined by
    a. a court of law.
    b. psychologists.
    c. psychiatrists.
    d. the DSM-IV-TR.

THERARIES

Psychotherapies are psychological techniques that can bring about positive changes in personality, behavior, or personal adjustment.
Medical therapies treat the physical causes of psychological disorders.

Mary Evans Picture Library/Photo Researchers, Inc.

Origins of Therapy

Historical evidence indicates that some form of treatment of abnormal behavior has existed since the Stone Age. Early treatments included crude surgical procedures and various superstitious treatments to combat supernatural forces. It wasn't until 1793, in Paris, that the emotionally disturbed were regarded as "mentally ill" and given compassionate treatment.

Psychotherapy Approaches

Although psychotherapies differ in orientation, they share certain features. Therapies may be conducted individually or in groups. Today, therapy may be conducted through the media, by telephone, or on the Internet.

How Effective Is Therapy?

Psychotherapy is not equally effective for all problems. The chance of recovery from some problems is good, whereas more complex problems can be difficult to solve. No single form of therapy is superior to others.

Medical Treatments

Most psychotherapists do not treat patients with major depressive disorders, schizophrenia, or other severe conditions. Major mental disorders are more often treated medically **(psychiatrists)**. All medical treatments have pros and cons.

Seeking Help

Most communities have a variety of services available for those seeking help with psychological problems. Awareness of how to locate these services is important. While practical considerations enter into the choice of a therapist, the therapist's personal characteristics are of equal importance.

Therapy Approaches

The major categories of psychotherapy are:
- **Psychodynamic** (based on Freud's theories)
- **Humanistic** (clients achieve a deeper understanding of their thoughts, emotions, and behaviors)
- **Behavioral** (the principles of learning and conditioning are used to make constructive changes in behavior)
- **Cognitive** (efforts are directed at changing maladaptive thoughts, beliefs, and feelings)

Characteristics of Effective Therapies

Effective psychotherapies share common elements: **a therapeutic alliance**, a protected setting, opportunity for insight and new perspectives, and a chance to practice new behaviors.

Somatic Therapies

Somatic (bodily) therapies include:
- **Pharmacotherapy** (use of drugs to treat disorders)
- **Electrical stimulation therapy** (altering electrical activity of brain)
- **Psychosurgery** (surgical alteration of the brain)

Therapies

Self-Management

Professional help should be sought when a significant problem exists. For lesser difficulties, it is possible to apply some behavioral principles yourself.

Cultural Issues

Differences in language, social class, values, and ways of communicating can have an impact on the effectiveness of therapy. Culturally aware therapists have the knowledge and skills needed to intervene successfully in the lives of clients from diverse cultural backgrounds.

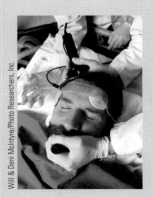

Chapter Concepts

- *Psychotherapy facilitates positive changes in personality, behavior, and adjustment.*
- *Before the development of modern therapies, superstition dominated attempts to treat psychological problems.*
- *Five major categories of psychotherapy are psychodynamic, insight, behavioral, cognitive, and group therapies.*
- *Psychotherapy is generally effective, although no single form of therapy is superior to others.*
- *All medical treatments for psychological disorders have pros and cons. Overall, however, their effectiveness is improving.*
- *Some personal problems can be successfully treated with self-management techniques.*
- *Everyone should know how to obtain high-quality mental health care in his or her community.*

Concept Review

1. Which type of therapy's goal is to lead clients to a deeper understanding of themselves?
   a. individual
   b. group
   c. insight
   d. action

2. Which type of therapy allows clients to assume responsibility for solving their own problems?
   a. directive
   b. nondirective
   c. time-limited
   d. supportive

3. Therapists in the positive psychology movement attempt to do which of the following?
   a. fix what is wrong
   b. help people make use of personal strengths
   c. passively solve problems
   d. none of the above

4. Eating tainted bread in the Middle Ages could have caused symptoms that were mistaken for madness in a condition called
   a. trepanning.
   b. demonological poisoning.
   c. ergotism.
   d. exorcism.

5. In psychoanalysis, unconscious conflicts may be revealed by
   a. free association.
   b. dream analysis.
   c. analysis of transference.
   d. all of the above

6. Which technique serves the purpose of lowering defenses so that unconscious material can emerge while a person is awake?
   a. free association
   b. dream analysis
   c. transference
   d. resistance

7. How does modern psychoanalysis differ from that of traditional psychoanalysis?
   a. Modern psychoanalysis requires a patient to meet with a therapist 3 to 5 times a week.
   b. It only focuses on the effects of the conscious in psychological disorders.
   c. Psychoanalysts are becoming greater in number.
   d. Modern therapists evoke emotional responses that will lower defenses and provide insights.

8. Client-centered therapy is an _____ therapy that is _____.
   a. insight; nondirective
   b. action; nondirective
   c. insight; directive
   d. action; directive

9. Betty's therapist looks shocked at something Betty has revealed. According to Rogers, the therapist has violated which of the four conditions of effective therapy?
   a. unconditional positive regard
   b. empathy
   c. authenticity
   d. reflection

10. Which of the following includes, as a key aspect, a technique called confrontation?
    a. psychoanalysis
    b. client-centered therapy
    c. Gestalt therapy
    d. existential therapy

11. Which type of therapy emphasizes immediate experiences and the integration of fragmented experiences?
    a. psychoanalysis
    b client-centered therapy
    c. Gestalt therapy
    d. existential therapy

12. Behavior therapists believe that people can change the way they are through
    a. insight into the causes of behavior.
    b. learning more appropriate responses.
    c. focusing on immediate experience.
    d. learning to think more logically.

13. Dr. Mason got sick on a hotdog while attending a baseball game. Since that day he has not been able to smell or eat a hotdog without feeling sick. This is an example of
    a. behavior modification.
    b. systematic desensitization.
    c. aversion therapy.
    d. virtual reality exposure.

14. Which term describes a process in which a hierarchy of fears, reciprocal inhibition, and relaxation are used?
    a. behavior modification
    b. systematic desensitization
    c. aversion therapy
    d. virtual reality exposure

15. Which of the following uses a computer to present fear stimuli to patients in a controlled fashion?
    a. behavior modification
    b. systematic desensitization
    c. aversion therapy
    d. virtual reality exposure

16. Which of the following is TRUE of EMDR?
    a. It is used to help ease posttraumatic stress.
    b. Clients are asked to visualize an unpleasant image while moving their eyes from side to side.
    c. It is used to treat generalized anxiety disorder.
    d. Clients are asked to visualize a pleasant image while engaging in muscle tension reduction.

17. Carrie used to give in to her toddler at the checkout line, buying the little boy a piece of candy so that he would stop crying for it. Now she remains firm and refuses to buy him the candy, no matter how much he cries for it. Carrie is trying to eliminate the crying with
    a. positive reinforcement.
    b. extinction.
    c. punishment.
    d. shaping.

18. Token economies have been effective with helping which of the following populations return to leading productive lives?
    a. mentally ill
    b. mentally retarded
    c. delinquents
    d. all of the above

19. According to cognitive therapists, _____ is a thinking error in which the person tends to perceive only certain stimuli in a larger array.
    a. selective perception
    b. overgeneralization
    c. all-or-nothing thinking
    d. heuristic reasoning

20. A depressed student who receives a "C" on an exam feels as though she is a complete failure. This is an example of what type of thinking error?
    a. selective perception
    b overgeneralization
    c. all-or-everything thinking
    d. "must" statement

21. Which of the following is NOT one of the three elements of REBT?
    a. activating experience
    b. emotional consequence
    c. anxious feelings
    d. irrational, unrealistic beliefs

22. In psychodrama, a client may observe someone else re-enact the client's behavior in a method called
    a. role-playing.
    b. role-reversal.
    c. mirror technique.
    d. cross-dressing.

23. Family therapy tends to
    a. be brief.
    b. be focused on specific problems.
    c. treat the family as a unit.
    d. all of the above

24. Generalizing from your text, which of the following is probably the most confrontational?
    a. sensitivity groups
    b. encounter groups
    c. large-group awareness training
    d. gender role groups

25. Sensitivity, encounter, and awareness group training
    a. tends to be a negative experience.
    b. may produce a therapy placebo effect.
    c. produces large benefits for clients.
    d. is best in corporate environments.

26. Research shows that about half of all patients feel better after only _____ therapy sessions.
    a. 8–10
    b. 13–18
    c. 26–36
    d. 50–75

27. Which of the following is NOT one of the eight goals of psychotherapy?
    a. ending unhappy relationships
    b. resolving conflicts
    c. restoring hope
    d. gaining insight

28. Which is NOT a characteristic of an effective therapist?
    a. is an enthusiastic listener
    b. is emotionally open
    c. values simplicity and clarity
    d. is mentally healthy and mature

29. If you are trying to comfort a friend in distress, one thing you should NOT do is
    a. listen actively.
    b. accept the person's point of reference.
    c. focus on feelings.
    d. give good advice.

30. Which of the following is a behavior that may hinder helping behavior?
    a. open-ended questioning
    b. opinionated statements
    c. silence
    d. genuineness

31. The process in which an electric current is sent through the brain for slightly less than a second is called
    a. pharmacotherapy.
    b. electroconvulsive therapy.
    c. psychosurgery.
    d. trepanation.

32. Major tranquilizers are also used as which type of drug?
    a. antipsychotics
    b. antidepressants
    c. antimanics
    d. mood-elevators

33. Which of the following is TRUE about ECT?
    a. ECT should be followed by the use of antidepressant drugs.
    b. ECT produces only temporary improvement.
    c. ECT may cause permanent memory damage.
    d. all of the above

34. Community mental health centers
    a. are the first step in hospitalization.
    b. have prevention as a second goal.
    c. provide long-term treatment.
    d. have some in-patient care.

35. Delia, who is trying to lose weight, is imagining herself at her ideal weight. In her fantasy, she is wearing a drop-dead gorgeous dress, and everyone is very complimentary to her. A man she likes tells her she looks fabulous. Delia is using the technique of
    a. covert sensitization.
    b. thought-stopping.
    c. covert reinforcement.
    d. desensitization.

SOCIAL THINKING AND SOCIAL INFLUENCE

Humans are social animals, living in a social world that often influences behavior. **Social psychology** is the study of how individuals behave, think, and feel in social situations.

Social Groups

We are born into a **culture** that provides a broad social context for behavior. Each person in a society is a member of many overlapping social groups; position in these groups defines roles. The presence of others may facilitate or inhibit individual performance.

Corbis/SuperStock

Attributions and Attitudes

Every day we must guess how people will act, often from small shreds of evidence. We do this through a process called attribution. Attitudes are learned dispositions that subtly affect almost all aspects of social behavior.

Intimate (0–1.5) Personal (1.5–4) Social (4–12) Public (12+)

Social Influence and Social Power

Social influence refers to changes in behavior induced by the actions of others. Influence ranges from mild (compliance) to strong (coercion). Social power refers to others' abilities to exert social influence through five types of social power: reward, coercive, legitimate, referent, and expert.

Group Characteristics

Social roles may be **ascribed** or **achieved**, and roles carry status. Destructive roles can override individual motives. Groups have standards of conduct, called **norms**, which can be formally or informally enforced. Group **structure** and **cohesion** influence behaviors in groups.

Fundamental Attribution Error

The most common error in judging others' behavior is to attribute their behaviors to internal causes (character flaws) when much of a person's behavior is based on external causes (the environment).

Attitudes

Attitudes consist of beliefs, emotions, and actions. They are formed through direct contact, interaction with others, child-rearing practices, and group pressures. The mass media and chance conditioning also play a role in attitude formation.

Conformity and Compliance

Broad social and cultural norms, as well as small group pressures, encourage conformity. Compulsive conformity in group decision making is called **groupthink**. Compliance involves more direct pressure to conform, and research finds that people often passively comply.

CHAPTER 16

Proxemics

Each of us maintains **personal space**, which is an extension of ourselves past the skin and into the environment. How close we are willing to allow others to get to us indicates the nature of the relationship with that person.

Persuasion

A deliberate attempt to change attitudes through information or arguments is persuasion. Effective persuasion involves likeable and believable communicators who repeat credible, emotion-arousing messages with clear-cut conclusions.

Attitude Change

Although attitudes are fairly stable, they do change. Significant personal experiences, reference groups, and deliberate persuasion have an effect on attitude.

Cognitive Dissonance

Inconsistency between thought and action can result in cognitive dissonance. This leads to attempts to reduce dissonance, often through attitude change.

Brainwashing

Forced attitude change is possible and depends on control of the target person's environment. This technique is sometimes used by coercive groups, like cults.

Greg Smith/Corbis

Social Thinking and Social Influence

Paul Chesley/Getty Images

Chapter Concepts

- *Social psychology studies how we behave, think, and feel in social situations.*
- *The nature of many relationships is revealed by the distance you are comfortable maintaining between yourself and another person.*
- *Social behavior cannot be fully understood unless we know what causes people attribute their behavior to and how they explain the behavior of others.*
- *A major fact of social life is that our behavior is influenced in numerous ways by the actions of other people.*
- *Everyone is affected by pressures to conform, obey, and comply. There are times when it is valuable to know how to recognize and resist such pressures.*

Obedience

Obedience is conformity to the demands of an authority figure. Many people demonstrate excessive obedience to authority.

Assertiveness

Assertiveness is clearly stating one's wants and needs to others, and it can be learned. Everyone is affected by pressures to conform, comply, and obey; it is valuable to recognize and resist these pressures at appropriate times.

Concept Review

1. Joe is an architectural draftsman. This is an example of
   a. an ascribed role.
   b. an achieved role.
   c. a cultural role.
   d. a group role.

2. Shannon has a big test in chemistry on the same day that her preschooler comes down with the chicken pox. We would expect Shannon to experience
   a. role conflict.
   b. role status.
   c. role anxiety.
   d. norm conflict.

3. The Stanford Prison Study conducted by Zimbardo and colleagues (1973) revealed the power of _____ in causing individuals to engage in destructive behavior.
   a. conformity
   b. obedience
   c. social roles
   d. prejudice

4. The degree to which members of a group are committed to remaining in the group is called
   a. group conflict.
   b. group structure.
   c. group cohesiveness.
   d. group adherence.

5. Which of the following is FALSE concerning in-groups and out-groups?
   a. In-groups can be defined on a variety of dimensions, such as race and sexual orientation.
   b. More positive qualities are usually attached to the out-group.
   c. Formation of in-groups and out-groups can set the stage for prejudice
   d. People tend to exaggerate the differences between in-groups and out-groups.

6. The idea that a stationary point of light in a completely darkened room appears as though it is moving is referred to as a(n)
   a. social influence.
   b. autokinetic effect.
   c. perceptual drift.
   d. social norm.

7. The distance at which impersonal business and casual gatherings take place is referred to as _____ distance.
   a. intimate
   b. personal
   c. social
   d. public

8. Which space term applies to formal interactions?
   a. intimate
   b. personal
   c. social
   d. public

9. Attitudes are expressed through
   a. beliefs.
   b. actions.
   c. emotions.
   d. all of the above

10. You are worried because your teacher seems to dislike you. Other students tell you that she treats everybody the same way she treats you, and you feel better. This illustrates the _____ component of making attributions.
    a. consistency
    b. distinctiveness
    c. situational demand
    d. discounting

11. Which term applies to the tendency to think that people in the audiences of infomercials applaud wildly because they are getting paid to do so?
    a. consistency
    b. distinctiveness
    c. situational demand
    d. discounting

12. A student who is afraid of not making a sports team overpractices to the point of exhaustion the day before tryouts. If the student does not make the team, he can attribute his failure to his exhaustion rather than to his lack of athletic ability. This student has engaged in what?
    a. the fundamental attribution error
    b. actor-observer bias
    c. self-handicapping
    d. distinctiveness

13. When we attribute the actions of others to internal causes, we are experiencing
    a. the fundamental attribution error.
    b. consensus.
    c. actor-observer bias.
    d. the double standard.

14. Which term refers to the tendency to attribute our own actions to external causes while attributing the actions of others to internal causes?
    a. the fundamental attrition effect
    b. consensus
    c. actor-observer bias
    d. the double standard

15. "I may not have the greatest job in the world, but at least I'm not unemployed like Mark" would be an example of a(n)
    a. social attribution.
    b. downward comparison.
    c. upward comparison.
    d. attribution.

16. Which measure of attitude allows people to freely express themselves on a particular topic?
    a. attitude scale
    b. personality assessment
    c. social distance scale
    d. open-ended interview

17. Any deliberate attempt to change attitudes or beliefs is known as
    a. conformity.
    b. compliance.
    c. persuasion.
    d. similarity.

18. *After buying a pair of shoes for more money than you had budgeted you experience emotional discomfort. This is an example of*
    a. showing incompetence.
    b. cognitive dissonance.
    c. overdisclosure.
    d. thought conflict.

19. *Which of the following is NOT a type of social power discussed in the text?*
    a. reward power
    b. coercive power
    c. expert power
    d. illegitimate power

20. *Pete notices that he runs faster when others are present. This improved performance might be explained by*
    a. social facilitation.
    b. social performance.
    c. comparison functions.
    d. performance dissonance.

21. *Although each person on the tug-of-war team could pull their own weight, the overall strength of the team was less than the accumulative weights. This might be explained by the idea of experiencing*
    a. cognitive dissonance.
    b. social loafing.
    c. personal space.
    d. social facilitation.

22. *Compared with men, women prefer*
    a. slightly younger men.
    b. higher status partners.
    c. more physically attractive partners.
    d. controlling and authoritative partners.

23. *You stand on a street corner and look up. Pretty soon, other people nearby start looking up, too. This exemplifies*
    a. conformity.
    b. group pressure.
    c. group cohesiveness.
    d. groupthink.

24. *Who would be most susceptible to group pressure?*
    a. people who deal well with ambiguity
    b. people who are self-confident
    c. people who are anxious
    d. people who are very individualistic

25. *What percentage of participants in the Asch (1956) conformity study agreed with the wrong line estimates of confederates at least one time?*
    a. 50
    b. 33
    c. 75
    d. 90

26. *Which of the following is a way to prevent groupthink?*
    a. First, state the problem subjectively.
    b. Encourage authoritative decision-making.
    c. Have a devil's advocate from outside the group.
    d. State personal preferences from the start.

27. *Which of the following is a factor that may affect a person's degree of conformity with a group?*
    a. importance of the group
    b. unanimity of the group
    c. intelligence of the person
    d. both a and b

28. *What is it called if you are forced to change your beliefs against your will?*
    a. coercion
    b. conformity
    c. compliance
    d. obedience

29. *_____ refers to the tendency for people to change their behavior just because of the presence of other people.*
    a. Social presence
    b. Mere presence
    c. Cultural expectancy
    d. none of the above

30. *In recruiting efforts, cults use which of the following?*
    a. isolation
    b. deception
    c. fear
    d. all of the above

31. *How many of Milgram's subjects went "all the way" and were willing to administer 450 volts of shock to a learner?*
    a. 25%
    b. 40%
    c. 50%
    d. 65%

32. *Milgram found obedience to be least likely when the*
    a. subject was in the same room as the learner.
    b. subject was face-to-face with the learner.
    c. subject was given instructions over the phone.
    d. subject was in a different room from the learner.

33. *Kelli asked the person interested in her car to just sit in it. She then gave them the key and instructed them to start it up. Following this she had them take it for a quick drive around the block. Kelli appears to be using*
    a. the foot-in-the-door effect.
    b. the door-in-the-face effect.
    c. the low-ball technique.
    d. evening the odds.

34. *Telemarketers will often ask you to make a donation to charity. They might ask for $100, which you refuse to do. Then they ask if you would give a smaller amount—say, $20. You agree, even though you don't usually donate money over the telephone. This is called*
    a. the foot-in-the-door effect.
    b. the door-in-the-face effect.
    c. the low-ball technique.
    d. evening the odds.

35. *In Moriarty's study of passive compliance, _____ of the subjects said nothing when the accomplice cranked up the music to full volume.*
    a. 50%
    b. 65%
    c. 80%
    d. 1%

PROSOCIAL AND ANTISOCIAL BEHAVIOR

While social life is complex, consistent patterns can be found in positive and negative interactions with others.

Affiliation

A basic human trait is the desire to associate with other people, rooted in desires for approval, support, friendship, and information.

Groups and Social Exchange

Group membership fulfills needs for **social comparison**. **Social exchange** theory suggests that we maintain relationships in which perceived rewards exceed perceived costs.

Prosocial Behavior

Behavior toward others that is constructive and positive is known as prosocial behavior. Understanding and removing barriers to these behaviors can encourage acts of helping and **altruism**.

Bystander Intervention

Four decision points must be passed before a person gives help: noticing, defining an emergency, taking responsibility, and selecting a course of action.

Aggression

Actions carried out with the intention of harming another person are facts of life. However, they are not inevitable. Both biological and environmental factors help explain aggression.

Prejudice

Prejudice is a negative attitude held toward members of specific social groups, which can result in **discrimination** toward group members. Victims of **social stereotyping** can experience **stereotype threat**.

Development of Prejudice

Prejudice may be the result of **scapegoating**, may develop for personal reasons, or may develop through adherence to group norms. Prejudiced people tend to be **authoritarian** and **ethnocentric**.

Mary Kate Denny/PhotoEdit

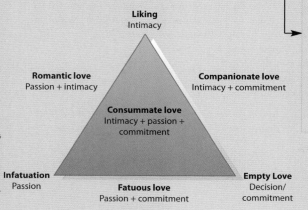

Liking
Intimacy

Romantic love
Passion + intimacy

Companionate love
Intimacy + commitment

Consummate love
Intimacy + passion + commitment

Infatuation
Passion

Fatuous love
Passion + commitment

Empty Love
Decision/ commitment

Adapted from Sternberg, 1988.

Prosocial and Antisocial Behavior

Interpersonal Attraction

Attraction is influenced by many factors, including proximity, frequency of contact, competence, similarity, and physical attraction. When two people like one another, they engage in more **self-disclosure**.

Relationships and Mate Selection

Adult love relationships tend to mirror **emotional attachment** patterns from infancy and early childhood. People typically select mates who are similar on many dimensions.

Triangular Love Theory

According to this theory, the type of love experienced depends on both partners' relative levels of **intimacy, passion,** and **commitment**.

Encouraging Helping

Helping is more common when there is **empathic arousal**, when the helper is in a good mood, if low risk or low effort is involved, and if there is perceived similarity between the helper and the victim.

Jonathan Nourok/PhotoEdit

Zefa/Corbis

Reducing Prejudice

Equal-status contact can reduce prejudice between groups in conflict. Focusing on **superordinate** goals can also be useful; **jigsaw classrooms** are an example of this. **Multi-cultural** harmony can be attained with conscious efforts to be more tolerant.

Chapter Concepts

- *We are attracted to other people—even potential mates—for reasons that are predictable and fairly universal.*
- *To persuade others, you must be aware of your role as a communicator, the characteristics of the audience, and the type of message that will appeal to them.*
- *Forced attitude change (brainwashing) is sometimes used by cults and other coercive groups.*
- *Prejudice, discrimination, intolerance, and stereotyping damage the lives of many people.*
- *Prejudice is reduced by equal-status contact with other groups and by mutual interdependence, which promotes cooperation.*
- *Aggression is a fact of life, but humans are not inevitably aggressive.*
- *Understanding and removing barriers to prosocial behavior can encourage acts of helping and altruism.*
- *Multicultural harmony is attainable through conscious efforts to be more tolerant.*

Concept Review

1. Terrence's desire to be around others is an example of what the text refers to as
   a. cognitive socialization.
   b. social desire.
   c. need to affiliate.
   d. social comparison.

2. Marcus found that when he played on a basketball team with players better than himself, he also improved his play. This is an example of
   a. downward comparison.
   b. introspective comparison.
   c. upward comparison.
   d. external comparison.

3. Mary and Saundra were best friends in high school. They were both only children with older parents, liked music and art, and were honor students. Their interpersonal attraction seems to be based on
   a. physical proximity.
   b. physical attractiveness.
   c. competence.
   d. similarity.

4. At a party, Richard was attracted to Katie at first, but as she talked, she revealed some very personal information about herself. Richard became uncomfortable and made an excuse to break away. Katie's mistake was
   a. showing incompetence.
   b. trying too hard.
   c. overdisclosure.
   d. self-disclosure.

5. Friendships between men tend to be based on
   a. activities they do together.
   b. feelings.
   c. confidences they share.
   d. self-revelation.

6. According to social exchange theory, if the _____ of a relationship exceed its _____, the relationship will probably end.
   a. rewards; cost
   b. costs; rewards
   c. comparison levels; rewards
   d. costs; comparison levels

7. Sternberg's triangular theory of love includes all of the following except
   a. passion.
   b. justification.
   c. commitment.
   d. intimacy.

8. People who want to be extremely close to their partners but are also troubled by doubts about the partner's dependability are experiencing
   a. secure attachment.
   b. avoidant attachment.
   c. ambivalent attachment.
   d. disorganized attachment.

9. When Dana was learning CPR she was taught to point at one person in the crowd and instruct them to call 911. She was told that by making one person responsible, rather than relying on the crowd, she would be more likely to get help and would decrease
   a. bystander apathy.
   b. bystander empathy.
   c. captive audience effect.
   d. none of the above

10. For a person to extend help to another they must first do what?
    a. Take responsibility.
    b. Define an emergency.
    c. Change.
    d. Notice.

11. Aggression, prejudice, and conflict are examples of
    a. prosocial behavior.
    b. antisocial behavior.
    c. illegal behavior.
    d. psychological compromise.

12. _____ refers to any action carried out with the intent of harming another person.
    a. Isolation
    b. Aggression
    c. Violence
    d. Dangerousness

13. Unequal treatment of people who should have the same rights as others is called
    a. prejudice.
    b. discrimination.
    c. scapegoating.
    d. replacement.

14. Which term refers to an attitude rather than a behavior?
    a. prejudice
    b. discrimination
    c. scapegoating
    d. replacement

15. Which term is a type of displaced aggression?
    a. prejudice
    b. discrimination
    c. scapegoating
    d. replacement

16. When you personally have no reason to dislike an out-group but your friends expect it of you, this is most likely
    a. personal prejudice.
    b. group prejudice.
    c. ethnocentrism.
    d. authoritarianism.

17. The focus on German superiority in Nazi Germany was an example of which of the following?
    a. personal prejudice
    b. individual prejudice
    c. ethnocentrism
    d. authoritativeness

18. The authoritarian personality
    a. is highly ethnocentric.
    b. was often severely punished as a child.
    c. is usually very dogmatic.
    d. all of the above

19. Social stereotypes
    a. are oversimplified images of people.
    b. are always negative.
    c. apply only to racial groups.
    d. apply only to ethnic groups.

20. *Stereotype threat is associated with all of the following EXCEPT*
    a. lower performance
    b. confirmation of the stereotype
    c. involving only racial groups
    d. making people feel threatened, especially in tasks involving ability

21. *In the experiment on prejudice using the eye color of children,*
    a. the in-group cooperated with the out-group.
    b. the in-group became vicious.
    c. the out-group was unaffected.
    d. the out-group maintained test scores.

22. *The experiment described in Question 21 demonstrated how quickly children can be influenced to hate one another based on*
    a. status inequalities.
    b. symbolic prejudice.
    c. equal-status contact.
    d. superordinate goals.

23. *An old science fiction novel's plot involves an imminent attack on Earth by powerful, mysterious aliens. The different factions and governments on Earth put aside their hostilities to cooperate in defeating the larger enemy. This is an example of which of the following?*
    a. status inequalities
    b. symbolic prejudice
    c. equal-status contact
    d. superordinate goals

24. *Which of the following is an example of a jigsaw classroom?*
    a. Each student contributing an essential "piece" to a group project.
    b. The more intelligent students in a class segregating from the less intelligent students.
    c. A mother, who is yelled at by her boss, coming home and yelling at her children.
    d. Students becoming fragmented from each other.

25. *Which of the following explanations for aggression has the least support?*
    a. aggression as instinct
    b. aggression as a result of biology
    c. aggression as a result of frustration
    d. aggression as social learning

26. *Reduced emotional sensitivity to violence is called*
    a. disinhibition.
    b. desensitization.
    c. sensory deprivation.
    d. dulled emotion.

27. *Which of the following is NOT one of the six ways parents can buffer the impact of TV?*
    a. Limit total viewing time.
    b. Closely monitor what is watched.
    c. Let children watch TV on their own.
    d. Discuss conflicts and violence shown.

28. *Equal-status contact*
    a. lessens prejudice.
    b. refers to interacting on an equal footing.
    c. often results in favorable changes in attitude toward others.
    d. all of the above

29. *To limit anger, which should people do?*
    a. Try only one primary alternative.
    b. Define the problem in general terms.
    c. Give all solutions equal weight.
    d. Choose a solution and try it.

30. *Which factor most affects the diffusion of responsibility?*
    a. how dangerous the situation is
    b. whether an authority figure is nearby
    c. whom the victim is
    d. how many people are present

31. *Giving equal status to different ethnic and racial groups while appreciating the differences is known as*
    a. multiculturalism.
    b. racism.
    c. human diversity.
    d. polynationalism.

32. *Individuating information refers to a focus on the*
    a. person.
    b. group.
    c. family.
    d. both a and b

33. *After Donn was fired from his job, Ray concluded that Donn must have been lazy and deserved to be let go. Ray's belief is an example of*
    a. social exchange.
    b. discrimination.
    c. victimism.
    d. just-world beliefs.

34. *If your psychology professor believes that everyone who sits in the back of the classroom is a poor student and acts in such a way that those students fail the class, we might suggest the presence of a*
    a. social competition.
    b. rivalry
    c. self-fulfilling prophesy.
    d. cultural error.

35. _____ *refers to the marriage of two people who are similar to one another.*
    a. Monogamy
    b. Interpersonal attraction
    c. Homogamy
    d. Romantic love

APPLIED PSYCHOLOGY

Applied psychology refers to the use of psychological principles and research methods to solve practical problems. Psychological principles have been successfully applied in diverse fields.

Cleo/PhotoEdit

Industrial/Organizational (I/O) Psychology

I/O psychologists study the behavior of people at work and in organizations. Applied, their work enhances the quality of work life through the training of leaders, better matching of people with jobs, and improving organizational structure.

Environmental Psychology

Environmental psychologists study and help solve problems related to physical environments (e.g., noise pollution), social environments (e.g., crowding), behavioral settings, and human **territoriality**.

Educational Psychology

Educational psychologists seek to understand how people learn and how teachers instruct to improve the quality of learning and teaching. **Direct instruction** and **discovery learning** are two teaching styles that yield different student outcomes.

Leadership

Leaders tend to be task-oriented **(Theory X)** or person-oriented **(Theory Y)**. Theory X is grounded in **scientific management** and is primarily concerned with **work efficiency**. Theory Y emphasizes **psychological efficiency** with methods like shared leadership, management by objectives, self-managed teams, and quality circles.

Environmental Problems

Environmental problems such as crowding, pollution, and wasted resources are based on human behavior. **Social dilemmas**, as well as overpopulation and overconsumption, contribute to these problems. Research shows that psychological strategies can be useful in promoting conservation.

Jury Selection

Who serves on a jury will affect the outcome of a trial. Psychologists often advise lawyers on which potential jurors should be selected or dismissed based on certain characteristics.

Psychology of Law

Psychological factors greatly affect the law and jury decisions. Studies of mock juries indicate that decisions made by juries are not always objective. Psychologists often serve in consulting and counseling roles in criminal justice settings.

Sports Psychology

Sports psychologists assist athletes by teaching them to relax, ignore distractions, or cope with their emotions to attain **peak performances**. Self-regulation strategies help focus attention and maintain optimal levels of arousal. **Task analyses** of sports skills help athletes and coaches improve performance of motor skills.

Human Factors

Ergonomists use **natural design** to devise machines and work environments that are compatible with sensory and motor capacities. **Usability testing** helps confirm that machines are easy to learn and use. Interesting applications in human factors include **human-computer interaction** and the design of space habitats.

CHAPTER 18

Job Satisfaction

Job satisfaction influences many factors that affect business efficiency, including productivity, absenteeism, morale, and employee turnover. **Job enrichment** can increase job satisfaction.

Yellow Dog Productions/Getty Images

Personnel Psychology

Personnel psychology is concerned with the testing, selection, placement, and promotion of employees. It begins with **job analysis** and includes the development and use of selection procedures like interviews, biodata, standardized psychological tests, and assessment centers.

AFP/Getty Images

Applied Psychology

SuperStock/SuperStock, Inc.

Chapter Concepts

- *Industrial/organizational psychologists enhance the quality of work by matching people with jobs and by improving human relations at work.*
- *Selecting the right person for a job or the right job for a person can be improved by using biographical information, interviews, and psychological tests.*
- *Effective management at work must take human behavior into account.*
- *Environmental psychologists study the relationship between environments and human behavior.*
- *Environmental problems such as crowding, pollution, and wasted resources are based on human behavior; they can only be solved by changing behavior patterns.*
- *Educational psychologists improve the quality of learning and teaching.*
- *Psychological factors greatly affect the law and jury decisions.*
- *Sports psychologists enhance sports performance and the value of participating in sports.*

Concept Review

1. The use of psychological principles and research methods to solve practical problems is called _____ psychology.
   a. applied
   b. industrial-organizational
   c. personnel
   d. job-analysis

2. Which type of psychology covers the major areas of testing, placement, and promotion of employees?
   a. applied
   b. industrial-organizational
   c. personnel
   d. job-analysis

3. Which is a method for evaluating job candidates?
   a. gathering biodata
   b. giving standardized intelligence tests
   c. performing a job analysis
   d. using the teaching center approach

4. Job enrichment usually leads to which of the following?
   a. increased absenteeism
   b. decreased job satisfaction
   c. increased production costs
   d. reduced boredom

5. In-basket tests and leaderless group discussions are both forms of _____ tests.
   a. vocational interest
   b. aptitude
   c. situational judgment
   d. multimedia

6. The management theory that assumes people are industrious, creative, and rewarded by challenging work is
   a. Theory X.
   b. Theory Y.
   c. Theory Z.
   d. Theory W.

7. A work group with a high degree of freedom with respect to how it achieves its goals is an example of
   a. participative management.
   b. management by objectives.
   c. a self-managed team.
   d. a quality circle.

8. Which of the following conditions is associated with positive moods created from high job satisfaction?
   a. less absenteeism
   b. better performance
   c. more creative problem solving
   d. all of the above

9. Every Friday afternoon the employees of Widgets, Inc., gather in the conference room to discuss ways to improve the quality of their product and services and to propose solutions to problems that have come up. This would be an example of
   a. participative management.
   b. management by objectives.
   c. a self-managed team.
   d. a quality circle.

10. _____ refers to a blend of customs, beliefs, values, attitudes, and rituals.
    a. Social culture
    b. Organizational culture
    c. Business environment
    d. Industrial society

11. Ileana was given the employee of the month award for her conscientiousness, courteousness, and willingness to be part of work meetings to better her organization. Ileana displays what the text refers to as
    a. work ethic.
    b. cultural defensiveness.
    c. industrial aptitude.
    d. organizational citizenship.

12. A church, an office, or a classroom would be an example of
    a. a behavioral setting.
    b. a physical environment.
    c. a social environment.
    d. a territorial environment.

13. Which of the following is TRUE about crowding?
    a. The world's population has become stable, with crowding becoming less of a problem over the years.
    b. Crowding makes it more likely for pregnancy to occur among a colony of rats.
    c. Crowding decreases aggressive behavior.
    d. Crowding is associated with an increase in stress-related illnesses among both animals and humans.

14. _____ refers to subjective feelings of being overstimulated by social inputs or a loss of privacy.
    a. Territoriality
    b. Crowding
    c. Attention overload
    d. Density

15. Research suggests that people are more likely to help a lost child if
    a. the child is male.
    b. the child asks loudly for help.
    c. the setting is a small town.
    d. the child is female.

16. The effects of daily exposure to noise include which of the following?
    a. lower blood pressure
    b. more persistence at intellectual tasks
    c. learned helplessness
    d. better school performance

17. The tragedy of the commons is an example of a(n)
    a. social dilemma.
    b. cultural conflict.
    c. environmental risk.
    d. escaping dilemma.

18. Which of the following is NOT one of the ways to encourage recycling?
    a. educate people
    b. provide monetary rewards
    c. give feedback
    d. discourage goal setting

19. *The study of the effects that buildings and their designs have on behavior using behavioral principles is called _____ psychology.*
   a. architectural
   b. environmental
   c. building
   d. organizational

20. *Dr. Jacob tries to stop during his lectures every now and then to ask if anyone has any questions. This would most likely be an example of which step in a teaching strategy?*
   a. learner preparation
   b. learner response
   c. evaluation
   d. spaced review

21. *The type of teaching style in which teachers create conditions that encourage learners to discover knowledge for themselves is*
   a. open teaching.
   b. discovery learning.
   c. direct instruction.
   d. Type A instruction.

22. *Which of the following is NOT typically part of direct instruction?*
   a. active discussion
   b. lecture
   c. demonstration
   d. rote practice

23. *Topics of special interest in the psychology of law include*
   a. conflict instigation.
   b. meditation.
   c. jury selection.
   d. judge appointment.

24. *Death-qualified jurors are*
   a. more likely to convict.
   b. more likely to be male.
   c. more likely to read criminal intent into one's behaviors.
   d. all of the above

25. *According to the text, which of the following statements about juror behavior is TRUE?*
   a. Jurors are less likely to find attractive defendants guilty than unattractive ones.
   b. Jurors tend to be swayed by the expertise of a witness rather than by the evidence.
   c. Jurors typically form a judgment early in the trial.
   d. all of the above

26. *The goal of sports psychology could be said to be to*
   a. create world-class athletes.
   b. understand and improve sports performance.
   c. involve more people in team sports.
   d. prescribe appropriate drugs to enhance winning performances.

27. *A _____ breaks complex sports skills into their subparts.*
   a. motor program
   b. motor skill
   c. task analysis
   d. peak performance

28. *_____ has also been referred to by sports psychologists as "flow".*
   a. Peak performance
   b. Intense concentration
   c. Elevated rehearsal
   d. none of the above

29. *Your college administration is performing a(n) _____ test for its computer lab by assessing the ease with which students can use the computers at their present desk heighth.*
   a. interactive
   b. usability
   c. protocol
   d. practicality

30. *_____ were designed to make us stronger, and _____ are meant to make us smarter.*
   a. Computers; machines
   b. Exercises; tests
   c. Machines; computers
   d. Assessments; controls

31. *Joshua is instructed by his coach to imagine his actions and behaviors for the upcoming game. This is an example of*
   a. a waste of time.
   b. mental practice.
   c. cognitive imagery.
   d. peak performance.

32. *Designing machines and work environments to be compatible with our senses and motor capacities is the goal of*
   a. natural assessment.
   b. human factor physiology.
   c. task analysis
   d. ergonomics.

33. *A motor _____ is a series of actions molded into a smooth and efficient performance.*
   a. skill
   b. program
   c. plan
   d. model

34. *Optimal skill learning involves all of the following EXCEPT*
   a. imitating a skilled mode
   b. getting feedback
   c. refraining from self-evaluation
   d. learning verbal rules

35. *Carl's job allows him to work four 10-hour days. This is an example of*
   a. flex time.
   b. a compressed workweek.
   c. telecommunication.
   d. down time.

BEHAVIORAL STATISTICS

Statistics allow us to summarize the results of psychological studies and draw valid conclusions about behavior. Statistics bring greater clarity and precision to psychological thought and research.

Graphical Statistics

Graphical statistics present numbers pictorially. Different types of graphs and tables show us the data in an organized manner.

Descriptive Statistics

To get a clear picture of how people behave, we often use descriptive statistics to organize and summarize numbers. This allows us to see trends and patterns in the results of psychological investigations.

Normal Distribution

Many psychological measures produce scores that form a **normal curve** (the bell curve). This is useful because the characteristics of normal curves are well known. When we chart the distribution of scores, we can visualize how well they conform to the expected distribution of scores.

Correlation

When there is a correlation, or a **consistent relationship**, between scores on two measures, knowing a person's score on one measure allows us to predict his or her score on the second measure.

Positive and Negative Correlations

A **positive correlation** exists when increases in one measure are matched by increases in another measure. A **negative correlation** exists when an increase in one measure results in a decrease in another measure. A negative correlation is not necessarily "bad."

Inferential Statistics

Some statistical techniques can be used to generalize results from samples to populations, to draw conclusions, and to tell if the results of a study could have occurred by chance. **Tests of statistical significance** indicate if the observed differences between groups are large enough to be improbable, suggesting that the results did not occur by chance alone.

Behavioral Statistics

Central Tendency

We often want to know the "typical" score in a group of scores. The **mean** is attained by adding all the scores and dividing the total by the number of scores (the average on your exam). The **median** is the point at which half the scores are higher and half are lower (half of you did better and half of you did worse on the exam). The **mode** is the score that occurs most frequently (the most common score on the test).

Measures of Variability

We also want to know how much scores vary. The **range** is the difference between the lowest and highest score. **Standard deviation** shows how much all scores in a group vary from the mean.

Standard Scores

Standard scores, or **z-scores**, give information about how far above or below the mean a score is. Since they use standard deviation units, they allow meaningful comparisons between scores from different groups.

Percent of Variance

By squaring the correlation coefficient, you can determine the amount of variability accounted for in the Y measure by knowing the X measure.

Causation vs. Correlation

Finding a correlation between two measures does not mean that one causes the other. Often two correlated measures are related due to the influence of a third variable.

Comstock Images/Jupiterimages

Chapter Concepts

- *The results of psychological studies are often expressed as numbers, which must be summarized and interpreted before they have any meaning.*
- *Summarizing numbers visually, by using various types of graphs, makes it easier to see trends and patterns in the results of psychological investigations.*
- *We usually want to know the "average" of a group of scores as well as how much they vary.*
- *Many psychological measures produce scores that form a normal curve. This is useful because the characteristics of normal curves are well known.*
- *Some statistical techniques can be used to generalize results from samples to populations, to draw conclusions, and to tell if the results of a study could have occurred by chance.*
- *When there is a correlation, or consistent relationship, between scores on two measures, knowing a person's score on one measure allows us to predict his or her score on the second measure.*

Concept Review

1. *Statistics that are used to summarize numbers and make them easier to communicate to others are called*
   a. descriptive statistics.
   b. inferential statistics.
   c. graphical statistics.
   d. variable statistics.

2. *In graphical statistics, a graph in which points are placed at the center of each class interval to indicate the number of scores and then connected by straight lines is called a*
   a. frequency distribution.
   b. histogram.
   c. frequency polygon.
   d. bar graph.

3. *Which is NOT a measure of central tendency?*
   a. mean
   b. median
   c. standard deviation
   d. mode

4. *Which measure is found by arranging scores from highest to lowest and then selecting the score that falls in the middle?*
   a. mean
   b. median
   c. standard deviation
   d. mode

5. *Which measure of variability involves the mean?*
   a. range
   b. standard deviation
   c. z-score
   d. both b and c

6. *On the normal curve, roughly 68% of all cases fall between _____ standard deviation(s) above and below the mean.*
   a. one
   b. two
   c. three
   d. four

7. *Which of the following is the largest group?*
   a. sample
   b. representative sample
   c. population
   d. representative population

8. *James wants to find out how lower-middle-class Americans feel about the president. He goes to the mall and stands outside one of the more expensive stores. His sample will probably be*
   a. too large.
   b. too small.
   c. representative.
   d. unrepresentative.

9. *Statistical significance refers to*
   a. how often experimental results could have occurred by chance alone.
   b. whether there is a difference between the experimental and control group.
   c. how much the scores within a group of participants differ.
   d. how well the scores in the experimental and control groups are related to one another.

10. *The number of hours you spend studying for your psychology test will (hopefully) be _____ with the grade you get on the test.*
    a. positively correlated
    b. negatively correlated
    c. uncorrelated
    d. weakly correlated

11. *The number of beers you consume while trying to study for your psychology test will probably be _____ with the grade you get on the test.*
    a. positively correlated
    b. negatively correlated
    c. uncorrelated
    d. weakly correlated

12. *If the points on a scatter diagram appear to form a fuzzy line going down from the upper left corner to the lower right, the correlation is*
    a. positive.
    b. negative.
    c. nonexistent.
    d. curvilinear.

13. *Which of the following indicates the strongest relationship?*
    a. $r = +0.78$
    b. $r = +0.12$
    c. $r = -0.89$
    d. $r = -0.23$

14. *For what are correlations particularly valuable?*
    a. determining causes of behavior
    b. making predictions
    c. analyzing open-ended data
    d. performing analyses of variance

15. *If you square the correlation coefficient, you get a number telling you the*
    a. percent of variable A that causes B.
    b. percent of variable B that causes A.
    c. percent variance.
    d. effect size.

16. *Causation*
    a. cannot be determined by an experiment.
    b. is difficult to prove.
    c. is the same as a perfect correlation.
    d. requires a survey to be performed.

17. *In a _____ sample, each member of the population has an equal chance of being included in the sample.*
    a. random
    b. subjective
    c. representative
    d. weakly correlated

18. *What type of statistics would be used to generalize survey results from a sample group to a population?*
    a. chance
    b. descriptive
    c. graphical
    d. inferential

19. *What is the range for the following test scores? 78, 98, 68, 83, 87*
    a. 82
    b. 45
    c. 30
    d. 15

20. *Normal curve refers to a(n) _____ distribution.*
    a. inverted V
    b. bell-shaped
    c. linear
    d. general

Answers to Concept Reviews

Chapter 1

1. *c*	8. *b*	15. *c*	22. *b*	29. *c*
2. *c*	9. *c*	16. *c*	23. *d*	30. *d*
3. *c*	10. *b*	17. *a*	24. *b*	31. *a*
4. *d*	11. *c*	18. *b*	25. *b*	32. *d*
5. *b*	12. *b*	19. *a*	26. *b*	33. *b*
6. *c*	13. *c*	20. *d*	27. *a*	34. *d*
7. *b*	14. *d*	21. *b*	28. *b*	35. *c*

Chapter 2

1. *c*	8. *a*	15. *c*	22. *b*	29. *d*
2. *b*	9. *d*	16. *b*	23. *d*	30. *c*
3. *a*	10. *a*	17. *a*	24. *a*	31. *a*
4. *b*	11. *c*	18. *c*	25. *c*	32. *d*
5. *b*	12. *b*	19. *c*	26. *b*	33. *a*
6. *d*	13. *b*	20. *a*	27. *c*	34. *c*
7. *a*	14. *d*	21. *c*	28. *a*	35. *d*

Chapter 3

1. *a*	8. *d*	15. *d*	22. *a*	29. *c*
2. *a*	9. *c*	16. *c*	23. *b*	30. *c*
3. *d*	10. *c*	17. *d*	24. *c*	31. *b*
4. *c*	11. *b*	18. *a*	25. *a*	32. *d*
5. *b*	12. *b*	19. *d*	26. *c*	33. *a*
6. *a*	13. *d*	20. *d*	27. *a*	34. *b*
7. *c*	14. *d*	21. *c*	28. *a*	35. *c*

Chapter 4

1. *b*	8. *a*	15. *b*	22. *c*	29. *c*
2. *b*	9. *b*	16. *d*	23. *a*	30. *c*
3. *b*	10. *b*	17. *a*	24. *c*	31. *a*
4. *d*	11. *d*	18. *b*	25. *a*	32. *d*
5. *c*	12. *d*	19. *a*	26. *d*	33. *c*
6. *a*	13. *b*	20. *a*	27. *d*	34. *c*
7. *a*	14. *a*	21. *d*	28. *c*	35. *b*

Chapter 5

1. *b*	8. *c*	15. *d*	22. *d*	29. *d*
2. *c*	9. *d*	16. *a*	23. *d*	30. *b*
3. *a*	10. *c*	17. *b*	24. *a*	31. *b*
4. *d*	11. *b*	18. *a*	25. *a*	32. *c*
5. *c*	12. *a*	19. *d*	26. *b*	33. *d*
6. *a*	13. *a*	20. *b*	27. *d*	34. *a*
7. *c*	14. *d*	21. *c*	28. *b*	35. *d*

Chapter 6

1. *a*	8. *c*	15. *b*	22. *c*	29. *d*
2. *d*	9. *c*	16. *b*	23. *c*	30. *d*
3. *c*	10. *a*	17. *b*	24. *c*	31. *a*
4. *a*	11. *a*	18. *b*	25. *a*	32. *d*
5. *d*	12. *c*	19. *d*	26. *b*	33. *d*
6. *b*	13. *d*	20. *c*	27. *a*	34. *b*
7. *a*	14. *a*	21. *a*	28. *d*	35. *b*

Chapter 7

1. *d*	8. *a*	15. *d*	22. *a*	29. *a*
2. *a*	9. *b*	16. *c*	23. *b*	30. *a*
3. *b*	10. *a*	17. *d*	24. *a*	31. *c*
4. *a*	11. *d*	18. *d*	25. *c*	32. *c*
5. *c*	12. *b*	19. *a*	26. *d*	33. *a*
6. *b*	13. *c*	20. *b*	27. *a*	34. *d*
7. *d*	14. *b*	21. *d*	28. *c*	35. *b*

Chapter 8

1. *b*	8. *a*	15. *d*	22. *a*	29. *d*
2. *a*	9. *b*	16. *c*	23. *c*	30. *b*
3. *d*	10. *c*	17. *a*	24. *c*	31. *c*
4. *d*	11. *b*	18. *b*	25. *d*	32. *a*
5. *d*	12. *a*	19. *c*	26. *b*	33. *b*
6. *b*	13. *b*	20. *a*	27. *c*	34. *d*
7. *d*	14. *b*	21. *a*	28. *c*	35. *d*

Chapter 9

1. *b*	8. *d*	15. *d*	22. *c*	29. *d*
2. *a*	9. *a*	16. *b*	23. *b*	30. *b*
3. *b*	10. *c*	17. *a*	24. *a*	31. *b*
4. *b*	11. *a*	18. *c*	25. *b*	32. *c*
5. *a*	12. *b*	19. *a*	26. *c*	33. *a*
6. *b*	13. *c*	20. *b*	27. *a*	34. *c*
7. *d*	14. *c*	21. *d*	28. *a*	35. *d*

Chapter 10

1. *d*	8. *d*	15. *c*	22. *a*	29. *d*
2. *b*	9. *a*	16. *b*	23. *d*	30. *c*
3. *a*	10. *c*	17. *a*	24. *b*	31. *d*
4. *c*	11. *b*	18. *c*	25. *a*	32. *b*
5. *b*	12. *b*	19. *d*	26. *c*	33. *c*
6. *c*	13. *a*	20. *b*	27. *b*	34. *d*
7. *c*	14. *c*	21. *b*	28. *a*	35. *d*

Chapter 11

1. *b*	8. *a*	15. *c*	22. *c*	29. *d*
2. *c*	9. *d*	16. *c*	23. *d*	30. *d*
3. *a*	10. *a*	17. *d*	24. *b*	31. *b*
4. *b*	11. *d*	18. *b*	25. *a*	32. *c*
5. *b*	12. *d*	19. *b*	26. *b*	33. *b*
6. *d*	13. *b*	20. *a*	27. *a*	34. *d*
7. *c*	14. *a*	21. *b*	28. *d*	35. *a*

Chapter 12

1. *c*	8. *b*	15. *a*	22. *c*	29. *b*
2. *b*	9. *b*	16. *b*	23. *d*	30. *b*
3. *b*	10. *c*	17. *c*	24. *b*	31. *c*
4. *d*	11. *d*	18. *c*	25. *a*	32. *d*
5. *a*	12. *b*	19. *d*	26. *c*	33. *b*
6. *d*	13. *a*	20. *a*	27. *b*	34. *d*
7. *c*	14. *b*	21. *b*	28. *d*	35. *c*

Chapter 13

1. *a*	8. *d*	15. *c*	22. *a*	29. *a*
2. *c*	9. *b*	16. *d*	23. *c*	30. *a*
3. *a*	10. *b*	17. *a*	24. *c*	31. *b*
4. *d*	11. *a*	18. *d*	25. *d*	32. *c*
5. *b*	12. *b*	19. *c*	26. *c*	33. *b*
6. *b*	13. *a*	20. *d*	27. *c*	34. *a*
7. *a*	14. *c*	21. *a*	28. *c*	35. *c*

Chapter 14

1. *a*	8. *d*	15. *d*	22. *a*	29. *c*
2. *b*	9. *c*	16. *b*	23. *c*	30. *d*
3. *c*	10. *c*	17. *c*	24. *a*	31. *c*
4. *d*	11. *d*	18. *c*	25. *b*	32. *b*
5. *b*	12. *a*	19. *d*	26. *b*	33. *c*
6. *c*	13. *d*	20. *d*	27. *b*	34. *b*
7. *a*	14. *c*	21. *c*	28. *d*	35. *a*

Chapter 15

1. *c*	8. *a*	15. *d*	22. *c*	29. *d*
2. *d*	9. *a*	16. *b*	23. *d*	30. *b*
3. *b*	10. *d*	17. *b*	24. *c*	31. *b*
4. *c*	11. *c*	18. *d*	25. *b*	32. *a*
5. *d*	12. *b*	19. *a*	26. *b*	33. *d*
6. *a*	13. *c*	20. *b*	27. *a*	34. *b*
7. *d*	14. *b*	21. *c*	28. *c*	35. *c*

Chapter 16

1. *b*	8. *d*	15. *b*	22. *b*	29. *b*
2. *a*	9. *d*	16. *d*	23. *a*	30. *d*
3. *c*	10. *a*	17. *c*	24. *c*	31. *d*
4. *c*	11. *c*	18. *b*	25. *c*	32. *c*
5. *b*	12. *c*	19. *d*	26. *c*	33. *a*
6. *b*	13. *a*	20. *a*	27. *d*	34. *b*
7. *c*	14. *c*	21. *b*	28. *a*	35. *c*

Chapter 17

1. *c*	8. *c*	15. *c*	22. *a*	29. *d*
2. *c*	9. *a*	16. *b*	23. *d*	30. *d*
3. *d*	10. *d*	17. *c*	24. *a*	31. *a*
4. *c*	11. *b*	18. *d*	25. *a*	32. *a*
5. *a*	12. *b*	19. *a*	26. *b*	33. *d*
6. *b*	13. *b*	20. *c*	27. *c*	34. *c*
7. *b*	14. *a*	21. *b*	28. *d*	35. *c*

Chapter 18

1. *a*	8. *d*	15. *c*	22. *a*	29. *b*
2. *c*	9. *d*	16. *c*	23. *c*	30. *c*
3. *a*	10. *b*	17. *a*	24. *d*	31. *b*
4. *d*	11. *d*	18. *d*	25. *d*	32. *d*
5. *c*	12. *a*	19. *a*	26. *b*	33. *a*
6. *b*	13. *d*	20. *b*	27. *c*	34. *c*
7. *c*	14. *b*	21. *b*	28. *a*	35. *b*

Appendix

1. *a*	5. *d*	9. *a*	13. *c*	17. *a*
2. *c*	6. *a*	10. *a*	14. *b*	18. *d*
3. *c*	7. *c*	11. *b*	15. *c*	19. *c*
4. *b*	8. *d*	12. *b*	16. *b*	20. *b*